Remembering Williamsburg

D1532665

Christopher Cheyne

Virginia women raised $400 in the 1890s to buy Williamsburg's Magazine, then called the Powder Horn.

Remembering Williamsburg

A Sentimental Journey through Three Centuries

By PARKE ROUSE, Jr.

DIETZ PRESS, *Richmond, Virginia*

Copyright 1989 Parke Rouse, Jr.

Printed in the United States of America

ISBN 0-87517-059-5

Cover photo: Bob Jones, Virginia Division of Tourism

Design by Stinely Associates

For five benefactors who treasured Williamsburg:

Cynthia Beverley Tucker Coleman

1832 – 1908

Mary Jeffrey Galt

1844 – 1922

Lyon Gardiner Tyler

1853 – 1935

William Archer Rutherfoord Goodwin

1869 – 1939

John Davison Rockefeller, Jr.

1874 – 1960

Contents

Introduction

WILLIAMSBURG has enjoyed two eras of unusual interest: first, its eight decades as capital of the colony of Virginia, from 1699 to 1780; and second, the years of its Restoration, beginning quietly in 1926 with John D. Rockefeller, Jr.'s unpublicized commitment to undertake a limited project and continuing, through the growth of the Colonial Williamsburg Foundation he created, till the present.

But what of "the lean years," between the moving of Virginia's government to Richmond in 1780 and the revival under Rockefeller's aegis since 1926? Until recently that era was largely ignored as a time of decay.

Inevitably, though, the miraculous regrowth of the College of William and Mary and of Williamsburg has focused attention on those "forgotten decades." Today we can see Williamsburg as a metaphor of Virginia's own history: a glorious colonial era, a decline from the Revolution through the Civil War, and a happy renaissance since the nightmare of Reconstruction.

Remembering Williamsburg is in a sense an outgrowth of research I have done for four books I have written. The first was *The City That Turned Back Time*, published by Colonial Williamsburg in 1952. The second was *James Blair of Virginia*, published by the University of North Carolina Press in 1971. The third was *Cows on the Campus*, an informal history of the town, published by Dietz Press in 1973. The last is *A House for a President*, subtitled "250 Years on the Campus of William and Mary," which I wrote for the college and which Dietz published in 1983.

I hope readers will enjoy these further glimpses of the old town and the part it has played in history.

Parke Rouse, Jr.
Williamsburg, Virginia

1

Colonial Williamsburg

Tobacco, early Virginia's mainstay, was shipped from the colony to Great Britain.

I.
From Plantation
to
Colonial Capital

1607 – 1787

British National Portrait Gallery

King James I ruled when British colonists in 1607 settled Jamestown and the Virginia Peninsula.

1. *The Rise of Middle Plantation*

WHEN Virginia chose Williamsburg as its capital in 1699, the British government was attempting to build up Virginia's towns and its trade with the mother country. A government dock and tobacco storehouses were built near town on Archer's Hope Creek, but over the next century they never drew as many ships as the more accessible ports of Yorktown and Hampton nearby. Even so, the old Williamsburg dock site is known and carefully preserved, and interest in it is growing.

I was present at the dock site, named Princess Anne Port in 1699, when work began in 1987 on a large residential area near there called Port Anne. Now the city of Williamsburg has created an adjoining six-acre nature park, preserving a site which housed a portside tavern in colonial times. There Williamsburg has built a green park with a catwalk over the creek-side marsh for sightseers and pleasure fishermen, a viewing platform, and parking.

Remote as this site seems, it is less than a mile from Williamsburg's Historic Area. Though the park is small, it commemorates the important fact that Virginia's eighteenth-century capital depended on British merchant ships to trade Tidewater tobacco for Britain's manufactured goods. Such was the mercantilist trade pattern of the British empire.

Jamestown on the James River had been the seat of government for Britain's first North American colony since its founding in 1607. But Jamestown's exposed and unhealthy location caused a removal to a more central capital at Middle Plantation, rechristened Williamsburg in honor of the king. It was only seven miles from Jamestown, in the middle of the Peninsula, but it was less swampy than Jamestown.

But the development in 1987 of Williamsburg's onetime port area created difficulties between the real estate developer of the new Port Anne cluster homes and established Williamsburgers, who opposed building a high-density residential area on historic acreage a stone's throw from old Williamsburg. After more than a year of hearings, a compromise—reducing the density—acceptable to Williamsburg's City Council was finally reached.

Before bulldozers began to level the pines and hardwoods that overgrew the area, a team of Colonial Williamsburg Foundation archaeol-

5

ogists, under staff archaeologist Marley Brown, made a survey of the 70 acres in hopes of saving any archaeological remains. They dug test pits in the hilly terrain, especially in areas where maps showed buildings may have stood, but nothing of importance has been found. The digging chiefly produced brick fragments plus bits of saltglaze and stoneware pottery from the colonial era.

Not much is yet known about the buildings which once stood at Williamsburg's chief dock area, whose creek name was changed in the eighteenth century from Archer's Hope to College Creek. The first dock was built after the 1699 Assembly act designating Williamsburg as the colony's capital had been passed. But it seems unlikely that the area developed greatly because the creek was so long and winding, from the James River to Williamsburg.

"Getting a sailing ship from the James River

Colonial Williamsburg

The sale of Virginia tobacco in England promoted the colony's growth.

to Williamsburg took a lot of valuable time," explained one local historian. "Sometimes the crew had to tow the vessel from a rowboat at the bow, which was slow and tortuous." The original name of Williamsburg's docks, Princess Anne Port, was given in honor of Anne of Denmark, sister of the late Queen Mary and soon to be queen herself.

The one or more government storehouses known to have been built at Port Anne were for the autumnal storage of hogsheads of tobacco, brought to the port by Williamsburg-area planters. One storehouse is known to have been owned at one time by John Greenhow, a Williamsburg merchant who shipped Virginia tobacco to Britain in exchange for manufactured goods, which he sold at his shop on Duke of Gloucester Street.

It is also known that taverns stood at Port Anne for the housing and entertainment of ships' crews and passengers while in port. There crew members and others could eat, drink, and while away time between ship arrivals and departures. For a while in the eighteenth century a small ferry—both sailed or rowed—operated from Port Anne to Hog Island on the south shore of the James River. It linked Williamsburg with lower Virginia and North Carolina.

Dissatisfaction with Williamsburg as a port helped fuel demands from Virginia lawmakers in the mid-1700s for a capital city more accessible to deepwater ships. Repeated efforts in the Virginia Assembly finally led in 1779 to the selection of Richmond as the new seat of government. The capital was moved there in 1780, leaving Williamsburg to decline until it was rediscovered by John D. Rockefeller, Jr. in 1926 and later restored.

In an effort to improve Williamsburg's water access, the General Assembly was asked in the 1770s to authorize the building of a canal through Williamsburg to connect College Creek and the James River with Queen's Creek and the York River. It was advocated also as a means of bringing northern and southern Virginia more rapidly together. However, the effort failed because of the potential expense and the onset of the Revolution.

At its zenith as a colonial capital in the 1760s, Williamsburg had several dozen merchants who depended on British imports for their stock-in-trade. For them and for the pub-lisher of Williamsburg's weekly *Virginia Gazette*, the arrival of British and European ships at Williamsburg's Port Anne in colonial times was an important event.

But it's good that Williamsburg's dock site is marked and preserved. It was once important to the little town's commerce.

William and Mary

William and Mary's original building partially burned in 1705 and was rebuilt. This sketch was drawn about 1702 by Francis Louis Michel.

2. *Samuel Mathews and Denbigh*

OF all the Peninsula plantations displaced by the upsurge of the years since 1607, the most fascinating to me is Denbigh, originally called "Mathews Manor." It was a royal grant to Capt. Samuel Mathews about 1626, and it was farmed until the 1950s. It is the point of land in north Newport News where the Warwick River joins the James.

In the 1960s, after the death of Mrs. Mackie Young Lane (Mrs. Spencer Lane of Williamsburg) and other Young heirs, the last 97 acres of the original 2,944 were sold to developer L. B. Weber. Weber got archaeologist Ivor Noël Hume of Williamsburg to excavate the foundation of the 1620s Elizabethan-style house, and then he divided his 97 acres into lots and sold them for residences. Called "Denbigh Plantation," it is today a Newport News suburb.

I visited Denbigh's river site first in the 1930s, when the elderly Miss Betty Young and her brother George lived there, almost as hermits, in a tiny kitchen of the second Denbigh plantation house. After their grandparents' mansion burned in 1871, the fortunes of the Youngs declined. Dr. Young, father of Mrs. Mackie Young Lane and others, then sold off chunks of his beautiful waterfront, some of it facing the James and some the Warwick River. They now make up Newport News's city penal farm and the Mennonite residential colony.

Denbigh's onetime Young's Lane—dirt in the 1930s—connects it with Menchville Road. The lane is now the axis of Weber's Denbigh development, flanked by East and West Governor Drive. The "Governor" honors Samuel Mathews, son of the colonizer, who became governor of Virginia as a young man in 1656–1660, while Oliver Cromwell was briefly Britain's ruler.

Denbigh's onetime layout was still partly visible when I went there in 1938, an alley between ancient boxwood trees, several terraces paralleling the river (perhaps created by Mathews for the mulberry trees in his abortive silkworm project), a tumbled-down stone dairy house, and the eighteenth-century kitchen where the last Young brother and sister lived.

Samuel Mathews chose his Denbigh plantation site because its Warwick River mouth offered a protected harbor for tobacco ships to and from England. A letter written from Virginia to England in 1648 called Mathews "an old planter of about thirty years standing, one of the (Governor's) Counsell and a most deserving

8

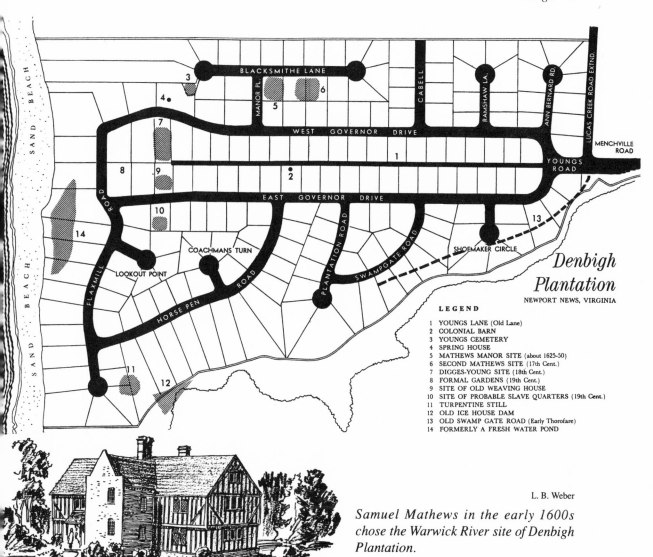

SAND BEACH

SAND BEACH

BLACKSMITHE LANE

MANOR PL

WEST GOVERNOR DRIVE

EAST GOVERNOR DRIVE

FLAXMILL ROAD

LOOKOUT POINT

COACHMANS TURN

HORSE PEN ROAD

PLANTATION ROAD

SWAMPGATE ROAD

SHOEMAKER CIRCLE

CABELL

RAMSHAW LA.

ANN BERNARD RD.

LUCAS CREEK ROAD EXTND.

MENCHVILLE ROAD

YOUNGS ROAD

Denbigh Plantation
NEWPORT NEWS, VIRGINIA

LEGEND

1 YOUNGS LANE (Old Lane)
2 COLONIAL BARN
3 YOUNGS CEMETERY
4 SPRING HOUSE
5 MATHEWS MANOR SITE (about 1625-50)
6 SECOND MATHEWS SITE (17th Cent.)
7 DIGGES-YOUNG SITE (18th Cent.)
8 FORMAL GARDENS (19th Cent.)
9 SITE OF OLD WEAVING HOUSE
10 SITE OF PROBABLE SLAVE QUARTERS (19th Cent.)
11 TURPENTINE STILL
12 OLD ICE HOUSE DAM
13 OLD SWAMP GATE ROAD (Early Thorofare)
14 FORMERLY A FRESH WATER POND

L. B. Weber

*Samuel Mathews in the early 1600s
chose the Warwick River site of Denbigh
Plantation.*

Commonwealths-man. . . . He hath a fine house and all things answerable to it, he sowes yeerly store of hempe and flax, and causes it to be spun; he keeps weavers and hath a tan-house, causes leather to be dressed, hath forty Negroe servants, brings them up to trades in his house; He yeerly sowes abundance of wheat, barley, etc. . . . hath abundance of kine, a brave dairy, swine great store, and poltery . . . he is worthy of much honor." A few gnarled mulberries still testify to Mathews's efforts to make silk.

When Warwick became one of Virginia's first eight shires in 1634, Mathews was one of its justices. Warwick court in early years was held at his house, which he called "Denbigh" for a county in Wales. The name spread and now embraces a growing Newport News area. Mathews or his son built a wharf, a boatyard for ship repair, and a rope walk. Nearby on Warwick River and on Mulberry Island lived other planters including the Carys, Pierces, Coles, and Blounts.

In Virginia, Mathews married the wealthy widow of Abraham Peirsey, and in 1653 he was sent back to England as agent for the colony. It is thought that he was still in England when his son, Samuel, Jr., became Virginia's governor at Jamestown, briefly replacing the royalist governor Sir William Berkeley. Both father and son were pro-Cromwell and anti-royalist.

The Digges family of York County acquired Denbigh plantation after the Mathews moved or died out. A second manor house, larger than the original Mathews manor, was built nearby, with wings and outbuildings added gradually. It was occupied by Diggeses for several generations. One occupant was Cole Digges, a prominent planter who became a member of the Governor's Council. The foundations of this house were excavated by Weber before he sold off Denbigh's lots in the 1960s. He found many curios.

The Youngs followed the Digges at Denbigh, and Young's millpond nearby survives from their ownership. When the Civil War erupted in 1861, Denbigh's owner William Young became a Confederate lieutenant and sent his wife and children as refugees to North Carolina. Denbigh plantation declined, along with the Peninsula, after the Civil War, especially after its manor house burned in 1871.

Dr. William Garrow Young, well-known late nineteenth-century Warwick physician, sold 1,200 of Denbigh's acres to the Mennonite families of Hertzler and Yoder in 1897. Dr. Young's son and daughter were the occupants of the place when I went there in 1938. They and others are buried in a family plot on the place.

As one of the earliest James River plantations and the designated site of a British shipping town in 1680, Denbigh's land and its foundations are important remnants of early America. We owe developer Weber (a Pennsylvania-born Mennonite who came here a half-century ago) thanks for his excavations and research before he cut up and sold this historic acreage. He and Noël Hume have put in writing a clearer picture of the farm village that Capt. Samuel Mathews "planted" in the 1620s, when Indians still roamed this Peninsula.

The brick wall of the second Green Spring mansion survived till this century, but is now gone.

Colonial Williamsburg

3. *Governor Berkeley's Castle*

SEVEN miles from Williamsburg, in the pines of James City County, lie the ruins of the most romantic house in Virginia. It's Green Spring, the seventeenth-century mansion of Sir William Berkeley. I like to think of it as the Versailles of Jamestown's day, scene of romance and intrigue.

Berkeley was the most durable and important of Virginia's seventeenth-century governors. He came to Jamestown in 1642 and ruled until deposed by Oliver Cromwell's Parliament in 1652. Then, after England's monarchy was restored in 1660 under King Charles II, Berkeley returned to Jamestown and ruled till his death.

A lot of the drama of Bacon's Rebellion in 1676, which clouded Sir William's last years, occurred at Green Spring. The governor once encamped 1,000 soldiers on its 5,000 acres. For a while it was a fortress.

But Green Spring is chiefly appealing to me as the earliest showplace in America, begun before 1650. Berkeley and his young wife, Lady Frances, lived like the English nobility they were. The Virginia Assembly met there several times in Berkeley's rule. Two later gov-

ernors, Lord Culpeper and Lord Effingham, lived there briefly.

Berkeley believed in impressing the public. As his widow wrote in 1678, he made Green Spring "the finest seat in America and the only tollerable place for a Governour." Most Americans then were lucky to have a tiny cottage. The Georgian mansions of Williamsburg and the James River were still 50 years in the future when Berkeley built his palace.

You wouldn't know any of that if you visited Green Spring's site today. It lies unnoticed along a rural James City County road close to Route 5 and Jamestown. The National Park Service in the 1950s acquired the site. The property is now fenced off and unidentified.

The foundations of the mansion, which the Park Service excavated in 1955–56, have been covered to protect against weather and souvenir hunters. The only structures standing are the tiny eighteenth-century jail and a springhouse. Someday the Park Service hopes to create an exhibit there. Historians have to separate the truth from the romantic legends that have grown up since the struggle between Berkeley and Nathaniel Bacon, who led the 1676 rebellion against him. The 1955–56 dig, led by Park

Service archaeologist Louis Caywood, revealed some new facts about Berkeley's house, but much still remains unknown.

Caywood's excavations showed that Berkeley's first house, dating from the 1640s, burned. It was evidently replaced by a much larger house about 1660, where the governor and his young bride lived during his second governorship. The house survived for more than 100 years after Berkeley's death as the seat of the Ludwell and Lee families, who were among the wealthiest in America. It was portrayed in a painting by an English architect, Benjamin Latrobe, about 1796, just before it was razed to make way for a new house.

The third and last house, built by William Ludwell Lee about 1800, was located a few yards away from Berkeley's house. After Lee died in 1803 without heirs, Green Spring passed out of the Berkeley-Ludwell-Lee line. Since 1803, Green Spring has been owned by a succession of buyers. The 1800 house has long since disappeared, and some of the Green Spring tract has been sold off. Most of the land today is in pine forest.

On the Park Service's Green Spring tract are a few other remains beside the house foundations, the jail, and the springhouse. Still standing is a brick wall from Governor Berkeley's orangery or greenhouse, where he grew orange trees imported from Spain. Still to be located are the remains of Berkeley's stables, barns, tobacco houses, and structures where his servants made wine, pottery, glassware, and collected fibers produced by silkworms from mulberry leaves grown there.

The most vital link surviving from Berkeley's day is the tiny freshwater spring that gives the place its name. It still bubbles away beneath the springhouse. Historians believe its drinkable water explains why Berkeley chose the spot, so far away from the James.

Green Spring's story begins in 1643, when Governor Berkeley arrived in Virginia from London and acquired 984 acres, "by name Green Spring," three miles north of Jamestown.

By 1664 he increased his plantation to 2,090 acres. In addition, he was given sole use by the Virginia Council of 3,000 acres of "Governor's Land" adjoining Green Spring.

The 1955–56 Park Service excavations revealed that Berkeley built his first house 68 feet wide and 70 feet long. It was big for that day and contained two brick towers and eight or nine ground floor rooms. Archaeologist Caywood believed it was two stories high and in Tudor or Gothic style.

Fire destroyed all or most of the house soon after it was built, archaeologist Caywood learned from the foundations. Then, apparently after his reappointment as governor in 1660, Berkeley began to rebuild and enlarge the house. He may have been encouraged to do so by his 36-year-old wife, Frances Culpeper Stephens, whom the bachelor governor married when he was 64.

Archaeologist Caywood surmised, "We may imagine that Sir William, before his marriage to Lady Frances in 1670, must have had a new feeling of social importance and could well have projected a new house. . . ." The new house was 100 feet long and from 35 to 55 feet wide. This was evidently the medieval-looking mansion painted by Benjamin Latrobe at Green Spring in 1796.

Paul Hudson, Williamsburg archaeologist and Park Service veteran, offers another insight about the house. "Green Spring," he has written, "must have been quite a pretentious structure, especially after Sir William's marriage in 1670. It obviously was furnished with the most elegant Stuart period furniture, glass, silver, pottery, and porcelain; as well as with fine fabrics and curtains, paintings and prints, and other accessories befitting a Virginia estate owned by a knighted friend of the king."

Besides trying to start new industries, Berkeley brought in European vegetables, fruits, and grains. He built formal flower gardens like those built by his English contemporaries. Latrobe's Green Spring painting shows curved walls perhaps defining a garden. Near the

By Benjamin Latrobe, courtesy Jamestown-Yorktown Foundation

Governor Sir William Berkeley built Green Spring near Jamestown in the seventeenth century.

house was the orangery or greenhouse, with three sides of glass and one of brick, the latter surviving. Like other Virginians, Berkeley found tobacco his best money crop and shipped it from Jamestown. He also had 1,500 apple, pear, and cherry trees "besides his apricocks, peaches, mellicotons, Quinces, Wardens [winter pears], and such like fruits." He experimented with rice, indigo, hemp, and flax. He imported racehorses from Ireland, bred his own racers, and staged quarterhorse races on Sundays. From England, the Earl of Clarendon observed that Berkeley had "a better subsistence than he could have found anywhere else."

Alas, when Nathaniel Bacon rebelled against him in 1676 Sir William's good days ended.

Though Berkeley finally triumphed, he returned to England in disrepute and died there in 1677. Three years later his young widow married Philip Ludwell I, whose son and grandson inherited Green Spring. The last Ludwell to live there was Hannah, daughter of Philip Ludwell III, who married William Lee of Stratford. It was their son, William Ludwell Lee, who razed the old house and built a new one.

Green Spring is long gone, but it deserves to be remembered. I hope someday the Park Service can open up the site to the public, with an exhibit kiosk containing pictures and a history of the Berkeleys, the Ludwells, and the Lees. A record of those high livers would make interesting reading.

4. *James Blair's Innovations*

SCOTTISH thought in the seventeenth century was exclusively monopolized by the pulpit," wrote John Malcolm Bulloch in his history of Aberdeen University. This obsession, which attracted so many able Scots to the ministry, was to be felt not only in the British Isles but in faraway America. Many an emigrant Scottish minister in the colonies played an important role in the American Revolution. When the Revolution finally burst, many Englishmen blamed the Scots. "There is no use crying about it," Horace Walpole wrote in England. "Cousin America has run off with a Presbyterian parson, and that is the end of it."

Of the early Scottish clerics in America, none exerted more lasting influence on America's intellectual growth than did James Blair, who founded the College of William and Mary and was acting governor of the colony. Sent out in 1685 by Henry Compton, Bishop of London, as a missionary, Blair before his death had unseated three royal governors and proved himself the ablest of men in governing colonial Virginia in the dawning years of her disaffection. The red-haired Scot was no man's man.

Though James Blair was more powerful in Virginia than his better-known contemporaries William Byrd and Colonel Robert "King" Carter, his posthumous fame declined for lack of such dynasties as theirs. Instead, Blair's marriage to temperamental Sarah Harrison, daughter of Benjamin Harrison II and collateral kinswoman of a signer of the Declaration and two presidents, was childless. As a result, the Blair papers and properties were dispersed. What was once a very passionate man thus became in time a rather bloodless myth.

But little by little over the years, facts and insights into Blair's career have come to light. They reveal him as much more than a political hatchet man who rose through his in-laws' influence. Paradoxically, he was a liberal churchman whose policies promoted the growth of congregationalism in Virginia, to the ultimate benefit of the Baptists and Methodists. He was likewise a whiggish advocate of colonial prerogatives despite his service for 56 years as commissary in Virginia to the Bishop of London.

He was also—there is no denying it—a skilled intriguer, who freely used his influence in church and state to obtain appointments and

Joseph and Margaret Muscarelle Museum,
College of William and Mary

James Blair was a Scottish missionary to Virginia who founded the College of William and Mary.

Joseph and Margaret Muscarelle Museum, William and Mary
Gift of Mary Monro Peachy

Sarah Harrison married James Blair but died young, without children, in 1713.

removals from office. In him survived something of the meddlesome church politician of medieval times.

The key to much of Blair is found in the ecclesiastical chaos which engulfed Scotland in his youth. Born in 1655 or 1656 during the Cromwellian protectorate, he spent his childhood in the rectory of Banffshire, where his father, Robert Blair, was Church of Scotland minister for 43 years. After schooling at home and probably in nearby Banff, he entered Marischal College in Aberdeen, later to be joined with King College as the University of Aberdeen. As he was only eleven or twelve when he entered Marischal, it seems probable that he was actually a preparatory student, aquiring the Latin and Greek precedent to university studies. In any case, we find him matriculating at Edinburgh in 1669, winning the master of arts from that institution four years

later, and then reading theology in Edinburgh under the Reverend William Keith and the Reverend Laurence Charteris.

Ordained in the Church of Scotland in 1679 by John Paterson, Bishop of Edinburgh, Blair was soon installed in the parish of Cranston, near Edinburgh. But the religious turmoil which affected Scotland then broke out again. For refusing to sign the Test Oath which was required of Scottish officialdom in advance of James II, Blair was turned out of his parish after three years' service, though Bishop Paterson had pronounced him a worthy and dedicated minister. To strong-willed James Blair and some eighty other ministers, the oath betokened a scheme to place the Roman Catholic King James at the head of the Scottish church.

To find places for Blair and other of his former students who had resigned, Laurence Charteris promptly wrote to Gilbert Burnet, a disillusioned Scot who had moved to London in 1673 and become preacher of the Rolls Chapel, a prestigious post within the gift of the Master of the Rolls, Sir Harbottle Grimston. Burnet obligingly agreed to help place them if they would come to England.

Accordingly, Blair on November 10, 1682, signed a document appointing his brother John, an apothecary in Edinburgh, to wind up his affairs in Scotland. Then he took the high road to London, there to become an under clerk of the Master of the Rolls on Chancery Lane, near Fleet Street. For such clerkships, Burnet thought England could "get so many good men, who suffered for their consciences, to be again well employed, and well provided for."

The Rolls Chapel had been built in the reign of Henry II as a chapel for Christianized Jews. Through Burnet, who was soon to become Bishop of Salisbury, Blair met many leading churchmen. Among there were Edward Stillingfleet, who was to become Bishop of Worcester; William Lloyd, to become Bishop of St. Asaph, of Lichfield, and finally of Worcester; and John Tillotson, who in 1691 was chosen by King William as Archbishop of Canterbury.

Most important of all, Blair came to know Henry Compton, Bishop of London, who was a liberal churchman of Blair's sort. Since the spiritual oversight of England overseas was considered the responsibility of the Diocese of London, Compton needed clergymen willing to venture to the New World as missionaries. In this effort he recruited episcopally ordained clergy from among England's Huguenot, Scottish, and Irish refugees, as well as from the Church of England.

Having been ordained by a bishop of the Church of Scotland, Blair was accepted by Compton. In the summer of 1685, he packed a sea chest and boarded the ship *William* with 56 other passengers for Jamaica. His fare was paid from the customary 20 pounds received from the King's Bounty for overseas service. From Jamaica, which was then the hub of English power in the New World, he sailed again to Virginia and his

assigned Parish of Henrico, then the western frontier of a colony nearing 70,000 people.

Located a hundred miles up the winding James River from the Atlantic, Henrico Parish had only recently been claimed from the Indians. Blair debarked at Varina landing, named for a Venezuelan tobacco which flourished there, and moved into the glebe house and its tobaccolands. In common with all Church of England rectors in Virginia—then about 30—he also received from his parish yearly enough hogsheads of tobacco to yield approximately 80 pounds.

Up to this point James Blair's career had advanced slowly, but now the tempo increased. To the dismay of her parents, he soon persuaded 17-year-old Sarah Harrison to break her marriage contract to William Roscow and to marry him instead—a man of 31. Then he was appointed by Henry Compton as his commissary or deputy to direct the leaderless Virginia clergy. In this capacity he promptly revived a languishing dream for a college to educate Virginians and Marylanders, as well as to Christianize Indians and produce an American clergy. Such a college had sprouted in Massachusetts in 1636, but Harvard was no more accessible to Virginia than was Oxford. Besides, Massachusetts was too puritanical for most Virginians.

Blair's pursuit of a royal charter and endowment for his college was an epic of persistence. Playing on Queen Mary's zeal for good works, he brought pressure wherever he could through the bishops and merchants trading in Virginia, meanwhile collecting funds from the estate of scientist Robert Boyle, from sympathizers with the Indians, and from three pirates who sought forgiveness from their sins committed in Virginia waters.

When at last he was presented to William and Mary by Tillotson, now Archbishop of Canterbury, he offered his petition:

Please, Your Majesty, here is an humble supplication from the government of Virginia for your Majesty's charter to erect a free school and college for the education of their youth.

Virginia Historical Society

A little-known miniature shows Blair's stubborn and determined personality.

"Sir," William replied, "I am glad that colony is upon so good a design, and I will promote it to the best of my power."

Thus it began, but Blair had to lobby for nearly two years before his petition made its way through the Lords of Trade to the Lords of the Treasury, at last to reach the Surveyor and Auditor General of His Majesty's Plantations in America, the ubiquitous William Blathwayt.

Blair's tenacity at last won out, aided by rising English imperialism and colonial growth. In 1693 the college was chartered, and three years later it was built at Middle Plantation, seven miles from Jamestown. So pleased was the Assembly with the site that in 1699 it renamed it Williamsburg and removed the seat of the government there. From Williamsburg the mammoth colony, reaching northwestward to the Great Lakes, was governed until the capital was moved to Richmond in 1780.

Blair in Williamsburg exercised influence second only to the governor's. Not only was he president of the college for life but he remained the bishop's commissary and served by royal appointment as one of the twelve-man Council, the prestigious upper house of Virginia's Assembly.

Blair's parliamentary battles with Governors Sir Edmund Andros, Francis Nicholson, and Alexander Spotswood rocked Virginia repeatedly from 1692 until 1722. Though sometimes vitriolic and wrong-headed, he contributed to a Virginia leadership which at its best produced George Washington, Peyton Randolph, George Wythe, Thomas Jefferson, John Marshall, and James Monroe—all of them associated with the College of William and Mary during or after Blair's presidency.

In his efforts to unseat objectionable governors, Blair made several voyages to England. He knew and corresponded with John Locke, who advocated an enlightened colonialism. He was active in the Society for the Propagation of the Gospel and the Society for Promoting Christian Knowledge, both created to Christianize the overseas dominions. For the latter, Blair prepared a five-volume collection of his sermons as rector of Williamsburg's Bruton Parish, first published in 1722 as *Our Saviour's Divine Sermon on the Mount*. These reveal his concern with the spread of Quakers, dissenters, and agnostics in the colony and his desire to purify the Church of England.

Through his marriage, Blair was allied not only with the Harrisons, but with their connections: the Ludwells, Burwells, Carters, and others who dominated Virginia's government. Through seniority, Blair in 1740 served for ten months as acting governor while Colonel William Gooch led an abortive British military expedition against the Spanish stronghold Cartagena, in South America. With his younger brother, Dr. Archibald Blair, and his brother-in-law Philip Ludwell II, he set up a store which added substantially to the 10,000 pound estate he left at this death in 1743 at the age of 88. He was buried beside Sarah near the all-but-vanished Jamestown, now a favorite site for sightseers.

In the lore of early Virginia, Blair is remembered chiefly as the giant-killer who intimidated a succession of royal governors and sent others packing back to England. However, his true monument is the College of William and Mary, which has survived to spread throughout the United States some of the Christian humanism that he soaked up from the pulpit and classroom in seventeenth-century Scotland.

Conjectural elevation by William S. Pavlosky

The first William and Mary building of 1695 burned in 1699 and was replaced in 1715.

5. *Catesby's Fauna and Flora*

YOU may not have heard of Mark Catesby, but he's becoming a familiar name in America. He was an English naturalist who came across the Atlantic to Yorktown in 1717 and spent seven years in Virginia painting watercolors of birds and plants.

From this beginning Catesby went on to write and illustrate a book that became a minor classic. Today he's called "The Colonial Audubon." His hand-colored prints of Southern birds, which illustrate two volumes of his book, sell for up to $2,000 apiece. And a rare first edition copy of Catesby's book, titled *The Natural History of Carolina, Florida, and the Bahama Islands*, was recently offered for sale at $77,500.

Catesby is a romantic but shadowy figure. Colonial Williamsburg in 1964 made a movie about him, called *The Colonial Naturalist*. Recently *Southern Accents* magazine featured him in an article, "Behold the Birds of the Air."

Once in Williamsburg, Catesby contributed to the world's knowledge of what the American continent was like in the early 1700s. Until the 1960s, few people except naturalists knew his name.

What is known of Catesby is simple. He was a middle-class Englishman who came to Virginia with his sketchbooks to visit his sister, Elizabeth Cocke. She was the wife of Dr. William Cocke, secretary of the Virginia colony, in Williamsburg. Wrote his biographers, "He had gone to America with little more than a critical mind, a love of nature, and the hand of an untrained artist." He ended up a lot better.

The young scholar found Virginia so intriguing he stayed for a while. He was attracted by the New World birds, animals, reptiles, insects, and plants he found here. And he met Virginians interested in the same things. One was John Custis, who lived on Francis Street. Custis's daughter-in-law was Martha Dandridge Custis, who after the death of Daniel Parke Custis would marry George Washington. John Custis imported tulip bulbs from Holland. His portrait, holding a tulip, gave him the nickname "Tulip" Custis. He had a fine flower garden. The house, facing Francis Street on the former Eastern State Hospital grounds, has disappeared. The surviving "Custis Kitchen" is a nineteenth-century structure.

Another friend of Mark Catesby was William Byrd II of Westover, who mentions Catesby often in his diary. Like many other educated colonials, Byrd collected or wrote about Virginia plants and animals.

In his travels through Virginia, Catesby sketched birds, animals, and plants in their natural habitat. From Virginia, Catesby went back to England, but he later came back to the Carolinas, Florida, and the Bahamas in the years 1722 to 1726. After finally returning to England, he wrote his two-volume *Natural History.* The first volume was printed in 1731 and the second in 1743.

Catesby either colored the 230 prints of his first edition or supervised other artists who did. He included descriptions of 113 species. One critic has called it "the most significant work of natural history until that of John James Audubon, more than 100 years later." The *Natural History* went through several editions and revisions.

Born in 1683, Mark Catesby was 29 when he came to Virginia. He died in England in 1749, at 66.

Colonial Williamsburg

Catesby used wildflowers as background for his bobwhite illustration.

Colonial Williamsburg

Catesby's owl and other illustrations were hand-colored for his book.

Unlike artists before his time, Mark Catesby painted birds with native backgrounds of trees and plants. Wrote Joel and Jean Mattison in *Southern Accents,* "His work is even more outstanding when one considers that Catesby gathered the materials, drew the sketches, engraved the copperplates, and life-colored at least some of the final engravings himself."

Catesby wrote his *Natural History* a few years before Swedish botanist, Karl Linnaeus, had published his Linnaean system for classifying plants and animals scientifically in 1758. However, the Englishman distinguished and named his species by the best means available to him. That helped Linnaeus.

Catesby's paintings are admittedly less beautiful than those of Audubon a century later, but they make up for it partly in naïveté. Write the Mattisons, "His subjects are somewhat stiffly and self-consciously posed for their portraits. . . . There is little interplay between subject and environment. The redheaded woodpecker, for example, appears glued (with visible feet) to an unlikely small-sized trunk of stylized oak, complete with oversized acorns."

But the Mattisons attempt to explain Cateby's shortcomings by pointing out that "these birds all had to be drawn from dead specimens, and there is little in the artwork, however brilliant or original, that suggests life." Sometimes he painted specimens distorted by rigor mortis.

Mark Catesby was just a name to me when I came to Williamsburg to work for "the Restoration" in 1951. Then John D. Rockefeller, Jr., became interested in film footage of birds and animals taken out West by two nature photographers, Ty and Julie Hotchkiss, now of Williamsburg. Someone suggested, "Why not have the Hotchkisses photograph Virginia wildlife for a movie recreating the Williamsburg years of Mark Catesby?"

That's how *The Colonial Naturalist* was born. My former Washington and Lee professor, Lawrence Watkin, was brought East from California to write the screenplay, and the pic-

Colonial Williamsburg

Insouciant bluejay, titled "The Chatterer," is a popular Catesby painting.

ture was filmed in 1964. The Hotchkisses set up photography blinds in Tidewater fields, where they got excellent footage of birds and animals without scaring them off. *The Colonial Naturalist* was the result.

The 55-minute film was premiered in 1965, and it fanned interest in Catesby. True, Catesby's *Natural History of Carolina, Florida, and the Bahama Islands* may not bring the $750,000 which the original four-volume elephant edition of Audubon's *Birds of America* recently brought. But Catesby is gaining on Audubon.

Catesby was only one of many English, French, and Scandinavian naturalists of the eighteenth and nineteeth centuries who left us pictures of birds and animals of North America. Another was Alexander Wilson (1766–1813), who was born in Scotland and came to America after the Revolution.

In 1825–1829, naturalist P. John Selby published another important bird book, and in the next few decades John James Audubon produced his masterpieces. Like Catesby, Audubon spent most of his time in the South. He lived for a while in Louisiana and then in Key West, where his home is a museum.

In Audubon, wrote the Mattesons, "bird portrayal was honed to a fine artistic edge. Not only are the creatures accurately shown in scale, but they are also lifesized." Audubon is to birds what Rembrandt was to eighteenth-century man. He is the Great Master.

Audubon's original drawings are now owned by the New-York Historical Society, which bought them from Audubon's widow in 1863 for a mere $4,000. They are exhibited at the society's New York museum.

I suspect that Catesby and Audubon had a lot to do with the growth of popular interest in birds and their preservation. As a result of their pioneering, Rachel Carson found millions of receptive readers when she wrote *Silent Spring* in the 1960s and wakened America to the threat of pesticides. Since then, "the bird people" have proliferated.

Mark Catesby painted this waterfowl for his two-volume 1731 Natural History.

Colonial Williamsburg

6. *Quarterhorses and Thoroughbreds*

KENTUCKY may be America's top horse-breeding center today, but Virginia claimed that distinction until the nineteenth century. The first European thoroughbreds in America were brought to Tidewater Virginia in the eighteenth century. And the earliest American thoroughbred races were held over rustic tracks in towns like Williamsburg, Petersburg, Richmond, and Alexandria.

Even today, Virginia is one of the top half-dozen horse-breeding states, along with Kentucky, Maryland, Texas, and California. Though Virginia's laws against betting unfortunately closed Virginia commercial racetracks, there are still a lot of horse shows and hunt clubs in Northern Virginia, around Warrenton, Middleburg, Upperville, and Berryville.

The horses that Virginians cherish are called "thoroughbreds," from the successful breeding of Arabian stallions to English mares in England about 1700. The first three Arabians imported to England were called the Byerley, Godolphin, and Darley stallions for the men who owned them. From them descend many of the famous Derby and Newmarket champions of later years. Man o' War was one of them.

Virginia planters learned about the breed of thoroughbred horses in the years when Williamsburg was the colony's capital. A Scotch-Irish shipmaster, James Patton, who later settled in Rockbridge County, brought Bulle Rock, the first English thoroughbred champion, to Virginia in 1730. He started something.

In the 70 years from 1730 to 1800, at least 216 stallions were brought over on English ships to Williamsburg, Hampton, Yorktown, and other such ports. Fairfax Harrison, a nineteenth-century Virginian who wrote a book called *The Equine F.F.V.s,* listed the main Virginia race-horse breeders of colonial days as follows:

Carter of Shirley, Harrison of Brandon, Nelson of Yorktown, Wormeley of Rosegill, Booth of Gloucester County, Byrd of Westover, Tayloe of Mount Airy, Morton of Leedstown, Spotswood of Newport, Thornton of Stafford County, Brent of Richland, McCarty of Pope's Creek, Baylor of Newmarket, Burwell of Carter's Creek, Braxton of Elsing Green, Ambler of Jamestown, Ludwell of Green Spring, Cary of Ampthill, Harrison of

Berkeley, Randolph of Tuckahoe, Lightfoot of Charles City County, Bland of Cawsons, Baird of Hallsfield, Evans of Surry County, Lee of Stratford, Syme of Newcastle, and Fitzhugh of Chatham.

Almost until the Civil War, Virginia was unsurpassed as a center for thoroughbreds. Now we've taken a back seat in that respect to other states which permit parimutuel betting— New York, New Jersey, Maryland, Kentucky, Florida, California, and a few others. Virginia horse farms still produce champions like Secretariat and Hill Prince, bred at the Chenerys' Meadow Farm at Doswell. But the big-time

Author's collection

Monkey, an early Virginia import, was bought by Nathaniel Harrison in 1737.

Fearnought,

WHO is now perfectly recovered, and in high spirits, will cover the ensuing season at NEW-MARKET, at EIGHT POUNDS a mare. The money to be paid before the mares are taken away.

I　　　JOHN BAYLOR.

Newmarket, April 20, 1767.

Colonial Williamsburg

Fearnought, advertised in the Virginia Gazette, *sired many famous racehorses.*

action has moved to televised race meets like the Kentucky Derby, the Preakness in Maryland, and the Belmont Stakes in New York.

It was different in the 1700s, when Virginia was the most populous and important of Britain's colonies. In those years many Tidewater planters imported blooded stallions from Ireland and England and developed racing in places like Green Spring, Williamsburg, Yorktown, Gloucester, and Petersburg.

The main contribution of Virginia to American racing was the development of the quarter horse, a smaller and nimbler breed than thoroughbreds. A few quarter horse races are still

held at county fairs in Virginia, but such races center nowadays in Texas, California, and other states west of us. For the quarter horse has merged into the cow pony and the pinto pony of the Wild West. They are more popular there today than in Virginia.

Nearly everybody knows that the modern thoroughbred race horse results from the seventeenth-century mating of Turkish and Arabian stallions—lean and long-winded racers with slender bodies and heads—to sturdier-looking English and French mares. Relatively few people, however, know that Virginia's quarter horses were similarly developed from Irish "hobby" horse stallions and Virginia mares.

Quarter horses were the usual saddle horses and racers in Virginia before thoroughbreds became common. They go back to the importation by Governor Sir William Berkeley in 1666 of the first recorded Irish "hobby" horses in America. He bred them and raced them at Green Spring, his plantation near Jamestown, along Route 5. Tradition has it that Berkeley ran his nags each Sunday afternoon on a straightaway on the dirt road to Jamestown, now a secondary road.

"Hobby" horses and quarter horses are relatively small, and they're renowned for their easy "amble" or "pace," which suited them for use as planters' horses on Southern plantations. Their muscular hind legs also give them a quick getaway, plus the maneuverability that proves so necessary in Western cattle roundups. It's their short-term speed that makes them good quarter-mile racers.

Races at Green Spring and other plantations were run between two horses on a straight quarter mile track. Three such heats would be scheduled, the first winner of two heats taking the prize money. Williamsburg still preserves a Quarterpath Road, where such races were held in colonial years at the east end of town.

One of the earliest races on the Peninsula was run in 1674 in York County. It resulted in a fine for a tailor who was presumptuous enough to race his horse in a gentlemen's sporting event. The York court on September 10, 1674, fined one "James Bullocke, a Taylor. . . three thousand pounds of tobacco and caske, it being contrary to law for a Labourer to make a race, being a sport only for Gentlemen."

Many accounts of quarter races survive. They were usually held on "court days" in county seats, drawing blacks and whites to line the raceway. Betting was heavy. The racing stakes were often entrusted to a member of the county court (equivalent to our board of supervisors) or to the parish minister, for Anglican Virginia then accepted horse-racing and betting as innocent diversions.

When the Reverend Hugh Jones arrived in Williamsburg from England in the 1720s to teach at William and Mary, he was struck by the mania for horses and racing in Virginia. He wrote that "The common planters, leading easy lives, don't much admire labour, or any manly exercise except horse-racing, nor diversion, except cock-fighting, in which some greatly delight. . . . The saddle-horses, though not very large, are hardy, strong and fleet; and will pace naturally at a prodigious rate."

Before the Revolution, quarter horse breeding moved into Southside Virginia and up to the Piedmont, where new tobacco plantations were developing. John Randolph had a stud farm on his plantation on the Roanoke River in southern Virginia. Other Southside planters in Surry, Prince George, Mecklenburg, Halifax, and Brunswick counties had stallions whose services they advertised in Norfolk and Richmond newspapers.

Petersburg and Richmond developed annual nineteenth-century races. A Carolinian named

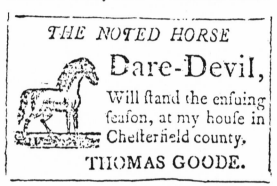

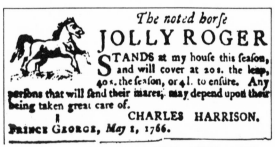

College of William and Mary
Virginia State Library

Eighteenth-century Virginians advertised stud services of thoroughbred stallions.

Marmaduke Johnson and two Mecklenburg County men named John Goode and Willie Jones became famous for their horses. Johnson's son, William Ransom Johnson of Petersburg, became known as "the Napoleon of the turf." His horses won high stakes North-South races several times in Washington, D.C. and New York.

When the Britisher J. F. D. Smyth visited Virginia in 1769, he was amazed by the popularity of quarter-horsing. "In the southern part of the colony," he wrote, "and in North Carolina, they are much attached to quarter-racing, which is always a match between two horses. . . and they have a breed that perform it with astonishing velocity. . . ."

Foremost among the quarter horses which set

Virginia Museum

Shark was an English thoroughbred brought to Virginia in 1786 by Benjamin Hyde.

records and became famous sires in Virginia were Janus and Sir Archy. In fact, the lineage of prized American quarter horses today goes back to Janus, which was brought to Tidewater from England in 1756. He was imported by a planter named Mordecai Booth of Gloucester County, who later sold him.

Beginning in 1737, a few wealthy Virginians also started importing thoroughbred stallions from England. Thereafter, oval racetracks were built in a few Virginia towns, modeled after the Newmarket track in England where rangy thoroughbreds raced for two, three, or four miles. That's the sort of horse racing most familiar across the nation today. Thoroughbreds have more "bottom" or endurance than quarter horses. They are the famous racehorses of our time though slower on the getaway than quarter horses.

The second thoroughbred stallion brought to Virginia was Monkey, imported by Benjamin Harrison of Brandon in Prince George County in 1737. Colonel John Spotswood of Spotsylvania County brought over another such stallion in 1751, and John DuVal of Henrico a third in 1756. These were bred to quarter horse mares throughout Virginia and North Carolina, creating blood lines which still show up in the genealogy of champion race horses.

The early nineteenth century was the heyday of racing in Virginia and North Carolina. Men like Jefferson, Madison, Monroe, John Randolph, Wade Hampton, and Patrick Henry went to races, even though the Virginia General Assembly in the 1790s began to restrict betting as contrary to public interest. That ultimately drove high-stake racing into Kentucky and Maryland.

So it seems that Virginia's role in the equine world will continue as the breeder of horses and the scene of steeplechase racing. Thus horses remain a part of Virginia life.

7. *William Byrd of Westover*

EVERY age produces its pace-setters. The most colorful one in Virginia before Jefferson was undoubtedly William Byrd II of Westover, a handsome hedonist who divided his time between London and Virginia, leaving a legacy of accomplishment as well as a scandalous diary.

No wonder historians call the aristocrat "The Black Swan of Westover." He was a dignified FFV, but how he carried on with the ladies! He was a man of two lives, indeed.

Byrd's life figured prominently in Williamsburg's history. He spent much time there. Byrd was one of Virginia's prime movers in the cultural upsurge that began with England's Glorious Revolution in 1688. Besides writing books and holding high office, he built Westover in 1730–31 and founded Richmond on his Henrico County land in 1737.

As a boy, Byrd was one of Virginia's many planters' sons to be sent to England to be educated—in Byrd's case as a lawyer. Several times after he inherited his father's land in 1704, he chanced the three months' Atlantic crossing. He loved London, its coffee houses, its Royal Exchange, its theaters, churches, and its Royal Society of scholars.

After Byrd's first wife, Lucy Parke, died of smallpox in London in 1716, the lonely widower stayed on there for a decade, rooming near the Strand and devoting part of his time to the search for a new wife. He returned to Virginia briefly in 1720–21, but he clearly preferred the worldly pleasures of London's court to the quiet life of Charles City County or even of Williamsburg.

Byrd described his womanizing in a secret shorthand diary that he kept for most of his life. The diary, now in the Huntington Library in California, was decoded and published in three volumes in the 1940s and 50s. It's America's closest equivalent to Samuel Pepys's delightful diary of Restoration London in 1660–69.

In his diary, Byrd describes casual acquaintances as well as his genteel pursuit of well-born heiresses. One of the latter was Mary Smith, whom he calls "Sabina" in his diary. She finally turned him down, her father disdaining Byrd's Virginia holdings. "I'd as soon own property on the moon," Papa scoffed.

The fashionable London of Byrd's day was a compact city of horse-drawn carriages and two-man sedan chairs. From Byrd's rooms near the Thames, he often walked to the London Ex-

Colonial Williamsburg

William Byrd built Westover on the James and also kept a house in Williamsburg.

change, where Virginia tobacco was traded. Nearby, on Threadneedle Street, was the Virginia Coffee House, where he dawdled with merchants and got news of Virginia from incoming travelers.

Byrd had family connections in London, where the Byrds had been goldsmiths before the first William had emigrated to Henrico County. Among other friends were young William's ex-schoolmates from Felstead Grammar School in Essex and the Middle Temple in London, where

he had studied law from 1692 to 1695. Among his friends in the city were playwright William Wycherley, poet William Congreve, and scientist Charles Boyle.

Byrd often went to court, then held in St. James's Palace, and at Whitehall. He frequently visited the village of Westminster, where Parliament sat. Still surviving at Chelsea is the Royal Hospital, built in 1681. At that time one of London's more prominent buildings, it was designed by Sir Christopher Wren and resembles the Wren Building at the College of William and Mary.

In his diary Byrd records attending many church services, sometimes criticizing the preacher and sermon. Among churches he frequented in London were St. Clement Danes, St. Martin's-in-the-Fields, both surviving, and the chapel in Somerset House near the Thames.

After the "Black Swan" succeeded in marrying the wealthy Maria Taylor in London in 1724, he brought her back to Westover and reared a second family of three girls and one boy.

In 1728, he was commissioned to survey the Virginia-North Carolina line, which he described in his *History of the Dividing Line*. He also wrote *A Progress to the Mines, A Journey to the Land of Eden,* and other scientific and literary works.

Despite his long sojourns in London, Byrd prospered as a Virginia planter. He settled a Huguenot colony on his Goochland lands early in the 1700s, obtained from the crown large western land grants, and became president of the Governor's Council in 1743 on the death of President James Blair of William and Mary, his lifelong political rival.

Thanks in part to his second marriage, Byrd had paid off all his debts by his death in 1744. In fact, he left his heirs 179,440 acres as well as Westover and other houses.

I find Byrd a fascinating complexity. Truly, he was a man of two worlds.

Colonial Williamsburg

William Byrd II of Westover lived life fully in London and Virginia.

Colonial Williamsburg

Evelyn Byrd, daughter of Westover's master, was courted, but never married.

Colonial Williamsburg

J. S. 'Jock' Darling III is Peter Pelham's successor as Bruton's organist.

8. *Peter Pelham, 'the Modern Orpheus'*

RTISTS and performers usually fare best in a leisured society, where kings or millionaires can sustain them with money. In early America, however, few men had sufficient wealth to be patrons of the arts until the industrial revolution wrought its great changes. Not until the nineteenth century did the United States produce a conspicuous harvest of painters, sculptors, musicians, novelists, and poets.

Music, the most convivial of the arts, was especially disadvantaged in Virginia. During its first century, the colony produced little except folk music to enliven nighttime revels. Then, with the planting of Williamsburg in 1699, a change began. The building of a college, the Governor's Palace, a theater, and a variety of inns and ordinaries created a setting for urban pursuits and gaiety.

Into this effervescent world in 1751 came a London-born musician who for the next half century would enliven Virginia with melodies both blithe and sad, both earthy and spiritual. He was Peter Pelham II, a 31-year-old organist and harpsichordist who moved into town in time to help install a pipe organ—the second in the colony—in Bruton Parish Church and to introduce to Virginia the soaring melodies of Handel, Vivaldi, Purcell, and other composers whose genius was resounding through the courts and churches of Europe.

Hundreds of Virginians and many a visiting Briton heard Master Pelham in eighteenth-century Williamsburg, and several left written testimony to his skill. In 1795, when the musician was 74 and still going strong, Judge St. George Tucker of Williamsburg took pen in hand to celebrate Bruton's "well-toned Organ" and its organist, "whose skill in his profession still secures him a small subscription from his fellow villagers, as well as a competent number of pupils for his support."

In refuting the Reverend Jedidiah Morse's aspersions upon Williamsburg in his *American Universal Geography*, published in Boston in 1793, Tucker wrote, "A week rarely passes in which a number of the inhabitants do not assemble for the purpose of passing an hour or two at church, while the ancient organist, or some of his pupils, perform upon this instrument; and often is the passerby invited into the place, in a fine evening, by hearing 'The pealing anthem swell the note of praise.'"

Tucker's estimate was confirmed by a visitor.

Wrote Alexander Macaulay, a native of Scotland, "Theres the Church fam'd for its noble Organ of one hundred tones, touch'd by the modern Orpheus—the inimitable Pelham."

Among Williamsburg's citizenry, Peter Pelham at first seemed a misfit. In a village of planters, collegians, shopkeepers, and slaves, a New England harpsichordist must have seemed out of place. However, Pelham's mildness and good nature soon ingratiated him. Besides, he was a well-educated and traveled man for his time. Born in London in 1721, he had moved with his father and two younger brothers to Boston after his mother died. Setting up shop in the Massachusetts capital about 1727, the elder Pelham taught reading, writing, dancing, painting on glass, and needlework. There the Pelham youngsters grew up.

The senior Peter Pelham is remembered for two reasons. First, he made some of the earliest American engravings before he died in 1751, many of them now in the Museum of Fine Art in Boston. His sitters were usually clergymen, ranging from the controversial Cotton Mather to the first president of Yale, Timothy Cutler. Pelham was credited with "an ability to paint excellent portraits as well as engrave them."

But the senior Pelham's second and greater claim to fame was his marriage in Boston to the widowed Mrs. Richard Copley. He thereby became stepfather to John Singleton Copley, who was destined to be the foremost painter in colonial America. Through Copley and through his artist son, Henry, born to his second wife, the immigrant Peter Pelham I enjoys an enhanced status in the graphic arts. "As the father of Henry Pelham and step-father of John Singleton Copley, and a colleague of John Smibert," declare the authors of *American Printmaking*, Pelham senior "exerted a decisive influence over the early development of the visual arts in this country."

In the Pelham-Copley household young Peter learned from his father to paint, dance, and to write a fine hand. Most of all, he learned music, which became the enthusiasm of his life.

In 1734, when he was 13, he left Boston for Newport as a student of "Charles Perchival," which was Pelham's spelling of Charles Theodore Pachelbel, a German organist and composer, and a son of Johann Pachelbel, whose music had influenced Johann Sebastian Bach in seventeenth-century Germany. With Pachelbel, Pelham studied music for nine years in New England and New York before going to Charleston, South Carolina, in 1737.

Pachelbel gave Pelham training in musical theory and composition as well as in harpsichord and organ technique, enabling him to do anything musical from composing, improvising, and arranging to installing one of the newly-introduced pipe organs. By 1741 young Pelham had become music master in the South Carolina household of planter John Fenwick.

Seeking a position as organist, Pelham returned to Boston in 1743. On May 30 of that year the *Boston Evening Post* carried the advertisement that "Mr. PETER PELHAM, Jun. who has been from Boston for these Nine Years past-, under the Tuition of an accomplish'd Professor of the Art of Musick, is now return'd; and ready to attend Ladies and Gentlemen as a Tutor in that Art on the Harpsichord or Spinet. . . ."

The young man fared well in Boston, aided by the good repute of his father. In November 1744, he was appointed organist of Trinity Church, where he helped set up and tune the organ. Two years later he married Anne Creese in that church, and as his family grew—eventually to number 14 children, eight of whom survived childhood—he needed more students and income. In 1749 he decided to move his family to Virginia, attracted by word that musicians there were few.

After settling several years in Hampton, where two sons were born, and briefly in Suffolk, where his daughter Sara was born, the Pelhams decided about 1754 to move to the more cultivated capital town of Williamsburg.

Though its population probably fell well short of 2,000 residents, Williamsburg was enlivened twice each year by Publick Times, a period of four weeks or more when the General Assembly and the principal court convened. During Publick Times officials and townspeople enjoyed theatricals, tavern life, balls, and horse races after the day's business. Peter Pelham evidently came to town to serve as conductor of the ensemble which played at Williamsburg's theater, the first in the colonies.

An ad in the *Virginia Gazette* in 1768 noted that John Gay's *The Beggar's Opera* would be performed, and "The musick of the opera [is] to be conducted by Mr. Pelham, and others." Meager though this was, it was an enviable opportunity for a musician in pre-Revolutionary Virginia.

Pelham was also hired by the vestry of Bruton Parish Church to help install the pipe organ which had been ordered from England several years earlier. The vestry had besought Virginia's governor and General Assembly for funds for an organ in 1744 as Bruton Parish served as the "court church" and the vestry deemed an organ "both ornamental and useful." After eight years' delay, a committee of John Blair I, president of the Governor's Council, Philip Ludwell III, Armistead Burwell, James Power, and Benjamin Powell was authorized to enlarge a gallery of the church and to install the desired instrument.

When the organ was finally in place, Peter Pelham was chosen to play it. With this appointment he became a conspicuous figure in Williamsburg's life for the remainder of the eighteenth century. It was a role he was to enjoy especially in the crucial pre-Revolutionary years, when Bruton Parish Church services were attended by such men as Edmund Randolph, George Wythe, George Mason, Benjamin Harrison, George Washington, Thomas Jefferson, and James Madison. To many a back-country Virginia burgess, the organ music of Bruton Parish must have been a first taste of the baroque glories of a new musical age.

Wrote young Anne Blair, daughter of Council president John Blair I, from the Blairs' house near the church:

. . . dear me I forgot to get those Song's I promis'd; well I will to Pelham on purpose for them this Evening.

. . . They are building a steeple to our Church, the Door's for that reason is open every day; and scarce an evening . . . but we are entertained with the performances of Felton's [William Felton, English clergyman and composer], Handel's, Vi-vally's [Vivaldi's] & & & &.

Despite such praise, Pelham's life in Williamsburg was plagued by constant need for money for his growing family. He was so pressed that in 1764 he decided to move to New York City, where he advertised his intention of establishing as a teacher of harpsichord, spinet, and thoroughbass. An advertisement he placed in a New York paper noted that he had taught for more than 20 years, 15 of them as an organist in Boston and Virginia, and that "the study, practice, and teaching of music [is] his only business." But students failed to appear in New York, and the next month he sailed back to Williamsburg.

Perhaps his brief absence proved his worth, for soon after his return he received a higher salary. In 1764, the Virginia Assembly and governor agreed to increase his stipend as Bruton's organist from 20 pounds a year to 30 pounds. The next year it was raised to 50 pounds. His growing stature also led some of Williamsburg's leading men to give him odd jobs for pay. He was frequently sought out for advice on music. Robert Carter of Westmoreland County, grandson of the famous "King" Carter, who was frequently in Williamsburg as a member of the Governor's Council, consulted Pelham several times before buying musical instruments.

It is also possible that Thomas Jefferson absorbed some of his taste for music from Peter Pelham. The red-haired Albemarle legislator declared music to be the favorite passion of his soul, and he developed a first-rate musical library at Monticello. In 1771 he wrote from there to Thomas Adams in London: "I have since seen a Forte-piano and am charmed with it. Send me this instrument then instead of the clavichord. Let the case be of fine mahogany, solid, not veneered."

Besides talent, Pelham apparently had charm of personality. He was described in various letters as an agreeable man, "sensible and very comical and entertaining," "extremely well liked," "behaves himself mightily well," "clever," and of "very good character." Not bad for a struggling musician!

Pelham arrived at an auspicious time in the emergence of music in Europe and the British Isles. The polyphonic style of the sixteenth century—the interweaving of two or more harmonizing melodies—had been developed by pioneer composers in Italy, France, and the Germanic lands. From the courts and churches of Europe's monarchs, new musical forms, harmonic structures, and instruments also were emerging. The opera, the oratorio, and the cantata had developed as vehicles for the voice, while the sonata, the concerto, the overture, the toccata, and the fugue had appeared for instrumentalists. Many works were being written for newly developed brass and woodwind instruments and for the pipe organ.

By the time Pelham ascended Bruton's choir loft, rococo and early classical musical styles were emerging. However, the cultural lag between Europe and America was so great that baroque music remained popular in the colonies through the eighteenth century after it had been succeeded by other styles in Europe. Peter Pelham performed many of these baroque works, some on the harpsichord and some on Bruton's organ. He also probably contributed lighter musical fare during the Williamsburg theatrical season, directed during a few years by the talented actor-manager Lewis Hallam, who brought his troupe from London, and after Hallam's death in 1755, by David Douglass, who married Hallam's widow.

Overtures, entr'acte music, and accompaniments were played by Pelham on the harpsi-

chord, augmented by available stringed instruments and "hautboys," which we know as oboes. The wind instrumentalists usually doubled on the flute or recorder. On one occasion, unnamed Williamsburg musicians played for "a grand tragic dance, compos'd by Monsieur Denoier, call'd 'The Royal Captive,' after the Turkish manner. . . ."

Music was an important feature of entertainments by the royal governor before the Revolution in the ballroom of the Governor's Palace. Leading planters from throughout the colony came to town for the annual king's birthday ball.

Each Sunday in his organ loft, Pelham accompanied Bruton's congregation in chants and psalms from *The Book of Common Prayer.* Forbidden by the Church of England in this period was the singing of hymns, which did not return to use in the established church until the nineteenth century, having been banned since Puritan times as "popish."

Despite this prohibition, however, hymns were widely sung in English households and in non-Anglican churches, like the Moravian and Lutheran. Among hymns popular in Pelham's lifetime were "O God Our Help in Ages Past," to a tune by William Croft, and "All People That on Earth Do Dwell," to the tune styled "Old Hundredth." In Pelham's period also came the powerful English hymns of Isaac Watts and of John and Charles Wesley, founders of the Methodist Movement, written to traditional secular melodies. Other hymns were translated from Germanic writers, whose fervent Protestantism voiced itself in a rich profusion of Lutheran and Moravian church hymns.

For a while Pelham kept a shop on Francis Street to make ends meet. There in 1768 he advertised a variety of notions and other goods in the *Virginia Gazette.* At another period he served as a committee clerk of the House of Burgesses, as he was one of Williamsburg's best-educated citizens. In 1771 he was appointed keeper of the colony's jail and moved his family into its keeper's house, close by the

Capitol. There Peter Pelham lived most of his remaining days, while his daughters married and his sons fought in the Revolution.

The spectacle of Pelham serving simultaneously as jailer, organist, and music teacher to young ladies has provoked some writers to laughter, but his contemporaries knew him as a substantial family man and a respected Mason along with Bishop James Madison, who was president of the College of William and Mary, and with Edmund Randolph, James Monroe, and St. George Tucker. On weekdays he doled out to prisoners their chores, meals, and punishments. Then on Sundays he would lead one of his trusted prisoners to Bruton Parish Church to pump the organ bellows while "the modern Orpheus" filled the church with music.

An occasional prisoner awaiting execution on Williamsburg's death row might also accompany Pelham to church, for colonial Virginia law directed the jailer to "carry all the prisoners under sentence of death to the Church . . . every Sunday between the Time of their condemnation and execution." On one occasion, after a series of jail breaks, Peter Pelham was accused of letting the jail keys fall into prisoners' hands. However, an investigation proved him innocent. Witnesses expressed "the highest opinion of Mr. Pelham's principles as a friend to American Freedom."

The Assembly's decision in 1780 to move Virginia's seat of government from Williamsburg to Richmond must have seemed a blow to Pelham's career. The move greatly diminished Bruton Parish's congregation, but Pelham remained in dwindling Williamsburg until most of his children had grown up and moved away. Wrote Benjamin Crowninshield in 1801: "The old organist, Mr. Pelham is removed to Richmond. He has been here about two years. His daughter Sara, who married the Reverend William Blagrave, took his place [as Bruton's organist] and was the last public performer. Since that time the organ has been falling to ruin." Williamsburg's golden age had clearly passed, along with Pelham's. In the nineteenth century, Bruton's "noble organ" was sold and removed to another church, to be replaced in Bruton only after decades of dire poverty in the old town. Pelham died in 1805, although the date, place, and burial site are unknown. It is thought he probably died at the home of one of his daughters in Richmond.

Not until recent years could the career of Peter Pelham be reconstructed, thanks to the restoration of Williamsburg. Today, once again, "a noble organ" graces Bruton Parish Church, and musicians versed in the eighteenth-century repertory perform frequently at the College of William and Mary and the Governor's Palace. A hitherto unknown Pelham minuet has been found and published, and a search continues for other compositions of this pioneer American virtuoso.

Indeed, the spirit of Master Pelham is very much alive in twentieth-century America. When the organ peals or the harpsichord tinkles in Williamsburg, you can almost visualize the little man in the gray wig, his head bobbing over the keyboard, bringing to life the deathless beauty to be found in music.

9. *Spotswood, the Builder*

WHEN Alexander Spotswood moved out of the Governor's Palace in Williamsburg in 1722 to make way for a successor, he went to rural Orange County and built a mansion, later burned and forgotten. Not until recently has Spotswood's "Enchanted Castle" been excavated by archaeologists. It has proven a major find and has touched off a $200,000 drive to save the site. Now Spotswood's house is the chief new challenge to Virginia preservationists.

I learned of the discovery recently from a descendant of the British colonel who governed Virginia from 1710 to 1722. Actually, Spotswood's house stood only from 1723 until it burned in 1740, the same year the ex-governor died. But in its brief life William Byrd II called the house an "enchanted castle," which has become its name. It was a splendid place, indeed.

You see, Spotswood was an able architect— the gifted eye that supervised the building of Williamsburg's Governor's Palace and gardens, Bruton Parish Church, and the Powder Magazine. Spotswood's army training in math and engineering helped him create the spacious beauty of Williamsburg's germinal years. His retirement house had the same charm.

Built overlooking the Rapidan River, near where Spotswood had established his earlier Germanna ironworks, the "Enchanted Castle" framed a 160-foot wide courtyard somewhat like that at the Governor's Palace. The house was flanked by two outbuildings and two advance buildings, all linked by what seems to have been a covered gallery.

Ivor Noël Hume, Colonial Williamsburg archaeologist, calls it "Virginia's most enigmatic and romantic building,"—enigmatic because no pictures and few clues survive of its appearance. Spotswood's writings about it were destroyed in 1859, when the Wren Building of the College of William and Mary burned.

Historic Gordonsville, a non-profit preservation group based in a nearby town, has raised $200,000 to buy 60 acres around the ruins and to protect the site. It lies along Virginia Route 3, halfway between Fredericksburg and Culpeper.

The "Enchanted Castle" began to reappear in 1969, when it was discovered during excavations for the state's Germanna Community College. A state archaeologist visited the site and confirmed that Spotswood had built it there.

Earlier, Spotswood as governor had named the nearby river "Rapid Anne" (now Rapidan), honoring the British monarch who had sent him to Virginia as her viceroy. He named many other Virginia sites.

The 1969 sampling of the site turned up several important artifacts. Eight years later, a team from the Virginia Research Center for Archaeology probed further and found the rear wall of Spotswood's house—the first hard evidence of the place.

When ownership of the land in 1984 passed to John Reynolds, a Culpeper businessman with plans to develop the area, the Historic Gordonsville group went to work to save the site. Subsequent digging turned up a 20-by-30 inch fireback made of cast iron and depicting Queen Anne. It is similar to a fireback found earlier near the President's House at William and Mary, both thought to have been cast at Spotswood's iron furnace at Massaponax, near Fredericksburg.

The 1984 dig also turned up detached dependencies near the main Spotswood mansion, including the kitchen. After they had found several chimney bases, archaeologists established that the main house had been 88 feet long —larger than the Governor's Palace.

The "Enchanted Castle" has become a Virginia landmark and is on the National Register of Historic Places. Architects say that Spotswood's architectural skill was surpassed in Virginia's colonial times only by Jefferson's. Some Spotswood enthusiasts would like to see a museum or an interpretive history-archaeology exhibit developed at the Castle.

Colonial Williamsburg

After Spotswood died, his widow, Anne Brayne, married an Anglican minister in Virginia.

After Spotswood died in 1740, his widow, the former Anne Butler Brayne, married an Anglican minister, John Thompson of St. Mark's Parish. They built a Georgian house named Salubria near the Enchanted Castle. That house still stands.

Whatever becomes of the new-found Spotswood mansion, it increases the evidence that he was one of Virginia's most remarkable colonial governors, along with Francis Fauquier, William Gooch, and Lord Botetourt. Too bad Spotswood in office had triggered the opposition of the Reverend James Blair. For Blair went to England in 1721, conferred with governmental leaders, and got Spotswood recalled. That ended his progressive 12-year governorship.

Today the foundations of Spotswood's Germanna house are exhibited under a shed to preserve them and a collection of artifacts uncovered, erected by Historic Gordonsville. The excavation was done by the Center for Historic Preservation at Mary Washington College.

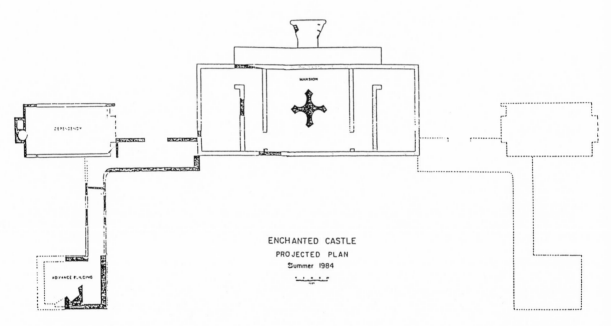

ENCHANTED CASTLE
PROJECTED PLAN
Summer 1984

Courtesy Kinsey Spotswood

Excavations of Alexander Spotswood's eighteenth-century "Enchanted Castle" suggest a house and four flanking buildings linked by a colonnade.

10. *Martha Custis and Her Kin*

MARTHA Washington, a onetime resident of Williamsburg, is the central figure in a small drama that is emerging these days. We will know more about Martha after a ledger and other Washington manuscripts, recently rediscovered at Washington and Lee University, are fully studied.

Meanwhile, William Abbot in Charlottesville, editor of *The Papers of George Washington*, says the W & L ledger "may be the most important addition to George Washington's material in more than a generation."

The story goes back to Washington's marriage to Martha, then the widowed Mrs. Daniel Custis, in New Kent County in 1759. By her first marriage she had two children, John Parke (known as "Jacky"), and Martha Parke, or "Patsy." She and the children inherited Custis's extensive property, which included a now-disappeared townhouse on Williamsburg's Francis Street, plus farmlands in New Kent, Northampton, Hanover, King William, York, and James City counties.

The new-found W & L ledger was kept by Washington for 12 years for his wife, who had been administrator of Daniel Custis's estate and

guardian of the children. Though he had been one of Virginia's wealthiest men, the 45-year-old Custis left no will. Under colonial law, his widow got a third of the estate and the children two-thirds.

Biographer Douglas Freeman wrote that the widow Custis "was among the wealthiest in Virginia when the tall young Colonel Washington bowed low to her on the 16th of March, 1758." After they married, Washington took over Martha's affairs and filed required estate reports with the Virginia General Court in Williamsburg. Washington administered the Custis property until his stepson, John Parke Custis, came of age in 1778.

The 36 leaves of the W & L ledger, written in Washington's firm script, are his record of his settlement of the Custis estate and his guardianship of his stepchildren. He submitted another copy to the General Court in Williamsburg, but it was destroyed by fire in Richmond in 1865 when state records were accidentally burned.

In Washington's ledger he recorded the income and expenses of his stepchildren's inheritance. As the basis for his record, Washington first copied the records that had been filed in court on Custis's death. They show that on his

Washington/Custis/Lee Collection,
Washington & Lee University

Col. John Custis IV moved to Williamsburg from the Eastern Shore and collected rare plants.

versity by Lee's daughter, Mary Custis Lee, in 1907. It remained almost forgotten in a university vault until taken out in 1983 by Lexington historians and studied. One of them, Joseph Horrell, then transcribed the ledger.

The Washington records cover 12 years, ending with Patsy Custis's death of epilepsy in 1773 and Jacky's engagement the same year. The records are especially welcomed by Editor Abbot of the George Washington papers project. "For the first time, we have a full account of Washington's handling of the affairs of his two stepchildren," Abbot says. "This was a very large estate and a good part of Washington's time was spent managing [it] during the 1760s."

The size of Martha Custis's estate has long been debated. Some of George Washington's critics have written that he married her for her money. However, Abbot points out that Washington was wealthy even before he wed the charming young widow. He really didn't need her six million dollars. In any case, the W & L discovery has been widely celebrated. A lot of human interest still lies in the Custis family and its fortune.

Meanwhile, speculation goes on in Williamsburg about the so-called "Six-Chimney House" that John Custis left to his son, Daniel Parke

death in 1757 Custis left property valued at 29,650 in Virginia pounds. The sum in today's money would be nearly six million dollars.

The rediscovered Washington ledger was inherited after Martha's death by George Washington Parke Custis, Martha's grandson, who is thought to have kept it at his Arlington House plantation on the Potomac River. After Virginia seceded in 1861, Custis's daughter, Mrs. Robert E. Lee, sent the ledger with other family heirlooms to Richmond and later to Lexington for safekeeping.

The Washington ledger was one of many Lee and Washington heirlooms given to Washington and Lee University by descendants of Robert E. Lee after he had served as its president from 1865 to 1870. The ledger was given to the Uni-

Drawing by John Millar

Delineator's conception of "Six Chimney House" in Williamsburg resembling Bacon's Castle in Jacobean style.

Custis. One interested scholar is John Millar, who has researched the Custises and their one-time Williamsburg dwelling.

John Millar likes to discover lost buildings. Brought up in Newport, Rhode Island, Millar graduated from Harvard in 1966, majoring in history. Since then the scholar has written several books, including *The Architects of the American Colonies* and *American Ships of the Colonial and Revolutionary Periods*. What brought Millar to Williamsburg in 1980 was his desire to study at William and Mary (he got his M.A. there in 1981) and to do research and writing.

That's where "the Six-Chimney House" comes in. Millar believes it was one of the most historic of Williamsburg houses and should be further researched and reconstructed. Located on Francis Street, the house was replaced in the nineteenth century by mental hospital buildings. Not only did Martha live there with her first husband, Daniel Parke Custis, but she is thought to have visited there with her second husband, George Washington. Some people even think George and Martha honeymooned there, but that is doubtful.

The building of the Custis house interests Millar even more than Washington's association with it. "I believe the house was built around 1675, when Williamsburg was still Middle Plantation," Millar says. "In fact, this may have been the 'Middle Plantation' referred to in the village's early name."

Millar points to the finding of archaeologist Ivor Noël Hume that the houses's six chimneys were actually sets of Jacobean chimneys at each end of the house, like those of Bacon's Castle in Surry. Hume reached that conclusion because General John Cocke wrote in the early nineteenth century that he copied his Jacobean-styled Bremo Recess in Fluvanna County "from the only two specimens of the like building I ever saw—the well remembered, old six-chimney house in Williamsburg and Bacon's Castle."

That pleases Millar, who wants to preserve quaint seventeenth-century-style buildings.

Washington/Custis/Lee Collection,
Washington & Lee University

After husband Daniel Parke Custis died, widow Martha married George.

"Six Chimneys" appeals to him as one of the few known Jacobean houses in North America, built in a Dutch fashion that gave way by 1700 to the more familiar English Georgian style.

Millar would like to see Colonial Williamsburg do additional research and then reconstruct the house. It sat on four acres fronting on Francis Street, a few hundred yards from the Public Hospital for the Insane, built in 1773 and just reconstructed by Colonial Williamsburg. The Francis Street property was bought by John Custis in 1714 and left on his death in 1749 to his son Daniel Parke Custis. Daniel lived there only eight years before he died and it passed to his widow, Martha. In 1778 John Parke Custis wrote his stepfather, Washington, that "Williamsburg is declining fast, & the House on my Lots are in a wratched [sic] condition."

After the Custises ceased to use "Six Chimneys," they leased it in 1762 to William Byrd

Washington/Custis/Lee Collection,
Washington & Lee University

Daniel Parke Custis inherited "Six Chimney House" from his father, John.

III, son of Westover's builder. In 1779, after George Washington had managed the property 20 years for his wife and stepson, it was sold to Dr. John McClurg, who taught medicine briefly at William and Mary. When McClurg moved to Richmond about 1784, Judge Samuel Tyler bought it and lived there.

Eastern State Hospital bought the four acres of "Custis-Square" in 1841 and built dormitories and a dining hall used by mental patients until 1959. Then the patients were moved to Williamsburg's west end and the state of Virginia transferred the Francis Street property to Colonial Williamsburg.

From his dig at the Custis house site in 1964, archaeologist Noël Hume concluded it consisted of a large central passage flanked on each side by a large room with a large Jacobean chimney. He believes it was probably a story and a half, like a house whose foundation survives at Jamestown, with Jacobean gable ends and clustered chimneys in rows of three.

Though George Washington was once said to have stayed at the Custis house when he came to Williamsburg in the 1760s to the House of Burgesses, that now seems doubtful. Washington's diary entries list room and board payments to Mrs. Campbell's tavern, now reconstructed.

Millar is also interested in the one-time horticulture of John Custis, who ordered plants from England for his garden at "Six Chimneys." As an amateur horticulturist, Custis knew Mark Catesby, John Bartram, and John Clayton. His correspondence with Peter Collinson, an English botanist, was collected by the late Earl G. Swem and published as *Brothers of the Spade*.

"'Six Chimneys' is a house worth rebuilding," Millar says. At present, however, Colonial Williamsburg has no plans to do so.

11. *Printing Comes to Virginia*

HOSTILITY between politicians and the press is nothing new. Since the time of that arch tory, Sir William Berkeley, who governed Virginia during Bacon's Rebellion in 1676, politicians have castigated the press. Berkeley wrote

> I thank God, there are no free schools nor printing [in Virginia], and I hope we shall not have these hundred years; for learning has brought disobedience, and heresy, and sects into the world, and printing has divulged them, and libels against the best government. God keep us from both.

The old governor was wrong, however. Free schools operated in Virginia even while Berkeley spoke, and printing came a few decades later. In 1730 a more liberal governor, William Gooch, permitted printer William Parks to move from Annapolis and set up a press in Williamsburg. It was Virginia's first. In 1736 Parks established his *Virginia Gazette*, a masthead that has survived despite many gaps until today.

We know little about William Parks, but he is important in history. Like Benjamin Franklin of Pennsylvania, he created a newspaper that was to inform colonists of what Britain and her colonies were up to. The two men helped create a sense of American unity and to bring on the Revolution.

William Parks's *Gazette* was a four-page government sheet that mixed proclamations and official pronouncements with "freshest Advices, Foreign and Domestick." Later colonial papers dared to be more independent. By 1776 Williamsburg had two *Virginia Gazette*s, one "loyalist" and the other "patriot." Freedom of the press was emerging, though slowly.

Parks was an enterprising man, born and educated in England. He drew a salary from Virginia's government of 120 pounds a year (later 280) as "public printer," to publish laws and government documents. His dormered frame printing shop on Duke of Gloucester Street, now exhibited in Williamsburg as the Printing Office, also served as Virginia's post office and as Williamsburg's bookshop, stationery, and book bindery. Parks and his family lived upstairs.

When ships from Europe reached Williamsburg, Yorktown, or Hampton, a post rider rushed London newspapers and mail to Parks's shop, where the printer held them for designees. News from abroad and other colonies was avidly received. Printer Parks would stop whatever he was doing to search the mails for news for his paper. When warranted, he printed an extra.

William Parks's *Gazette* office was a nerve center through which news from the world reached many scattered Virginians who by that time had strayed west as far as the Alleghenies. Other printers in other colonies did likewise. Thus eight or nine tiny newspapers up and down the Atlantic coast kept colonial leaders informed of the world in the 1730s and 40s. Many papers were passed around in taverns or posted in public places.

About 1743 Parks and his friend Benjamin Franklin started a paper mill just south of Williamsburg on what is now Paper Mill Creek. (The site is on the Colonial Parkway between Williamsburg and Jamestown.) Though Parks died in 1750 on a trip to England, his mill is thought to have survived a while after him. Its paper has been found in a German Bible and a songbook printed in Pennsylvania in 1763. Parks's watermark is valued by book collectors when it occasionally turns up as evidence of Williamsburg-made paper.

Parks was a man of judgment and taste. In the first issue of his *Virginia Gazette* in August of 1763, he wrote a "Printer's Introduction" promising to print no articles to create dissension or to attack politicians. Besides *Gazettes* and statutes, Parks in Williamsburg printed political and religious tracts, pamphlets, almanacs, and one or two hardbound books. He amplified his income as public printer by job printing, turning out blank forms for deeds, mortgages, and bills.

Although historians cherish the few precious surviving copies of Parks's *Gazette*, most readers today find them dull. Local events were rarely reported, except for occasional marriage and death notices. Lengthy Acts of the Assembly ran in full, without comment. Anonymous letter writers posed philosophical questions, using noms de plume to conceal identity. It was bad form in those days for a gentleman to "get in the paper."

Even so, hints of controversy began to build up as the revolutionary years approached. There were also notices of runaway slaves, strayed horses and cows, of deserted spouses, and of racing stallions standing at stud for a fee. From the ads, you could also learn of goods newly arrived from London—articles on sale in shops on Duke of Gloucester Street.

In one of his first issues, William Parks ran this appeal:

> All persons who have Occasion to buy or sell Horses, Cattle, & or want to give any Publick Notice; may have it advertis'd in all these Gazettes printed in one Week, for Three Shillings. . . .

Poetry often appeared in the *Virginia Gazette.* Parks also printed as pamphlets various poems and essays written by Virginians, especially professors at William and Mary. In a separate literary journal, "Virginia Miscellany," which he published for a brief period in 1730, he included among poems an ode which fulsomely saluted Governor Gooch for permitting the creation of Parks's press. It concluded:

> A Ruler's gentle Influence
> Shall o'er his Land be shewn;
> Saturnian Reigns shall be renew'd
> Truth, Justice, Vertue, be pursu'd
> Art flourish, Peace shall crown the Plains,
> Where GOOCH administers, AUGUSTUS
>   reigns.

After William Parks died in 1750, his assistant, William Hunter, bought his *Virginia Gazette.* Hunter also succeeded Parks as public printer and postmaster. Hunter and Benjamin Franklin in the 50s were both appointed deputy postmasters-general of the 13 colonies, and Ben came to Williamsburg to confer with Hunter on postal service.

Hunter endeared himself to posterity in 1754 by printing the first published writing of George Washington, titled "The Journal of Major George Washington, sent by the Hon. Robert Dinwiddie, Esq; His Majesty's Lieutenant-Gov-

Colonial Williamsburg

William Parks's 1736 Virginia Gazette *printery is exhibited for visitors.*

ernor, and Commander in Chief of Virginia, to the Commandant of the French Forces on Ohio. . . ." Only eight copies of the tiny book are known, all worth their weight in gold.

After Hunter died in 1761, the *Gazette* had a succession of owner-operators. When Virginians became disaffected with Britain, the role of public printer in Williamsburg became vexatious. Should he side with the loyalist governor or the rebellious assembly? Hunter's successor, Joseph Royle, caught hell in his five years as public printer before his death in 1766.

When Scotsman Alexander Purdie succeeded

Royle, he tried to stay in with both sides. However, a printer named William Rind came from Maryland to Williamsburg in 1766 and set up a competing paper, more sympathetic to colonial resistance than Purdie was. Thomas Jefferson, who was then in Williamsburg studying law, wrote that "We had but one press, and that having the whole business of the government, and no competitor for public favor, nothing disagreeable to the governor could be got into it. We procured Rind to come from Maryland to publish a free paper."

When Governor Jefferson in 1780 promoted

the move of the Virginia government from Williamsburg to Richmond, the two *Gazettes* went with it. The job of public printer was soon made nonpolitical so that no newspaper had an inside track to the state's printing or to its news.

Newspapers have come a long way since William Parks's *Gazette*. No longer are they state-sponsored supporters of the status quo but free agents. It's better that way.

Thomas Jefferson gained his first acquaintance with newspapers from Parks's *Gazette* and its successors. Jefferson, you recall, wrote: "Were it left to me to decide whether we should have a Government without Newspapers, or Newspapers without a Government, I should not hesitate to prefer the latter."

William Parks was a good editor and writer and evidently a good businessman. He pub-

lished several small books, all collectors' items today. He also imported British books.

The *Virginia Gazette's* history after 1780 is a complicated story. Williamsburg was without a paper until R. A. Lively revived the *Gazette* before the Civil War. When Federal forces invaded the town on May 5, 1862, Lively was imprisoned and his presses were impounded by the Union. After the Civil War the *Gazette* title languished until William and Mary tried to revive it in 1926 and J. A. Osborne did so in 1930. His family ran it until the late John O. W. Gravely III bought it in 1960. Gravely's widow has subsequently sold it.

As Jefferson said, a democratic people needs good newspapers to inform them. That's what the *Gazette* seems to be doing.

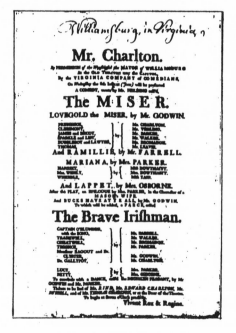

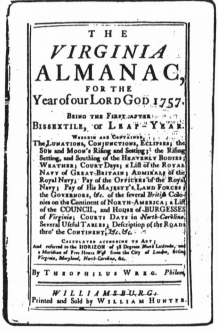

Colonial Williamsburg

Playbills and almanacs were among the products of Williamsburg's early printers.

12. *Treating Disordered Minds*

VIRGINIA had only a few doctors from Jamestown's day till this century, and medical knowledge was skimpy. One of the best doctors in early Williamsburg was a Sephardic Jew of Portuguese extraction, John de Sequeyra, who came to town about 1745 and lived there until he died in 1795. During 22 of those years he was the visiting physician at the Lunatic Asylum, now Eastern State Hospital, and served also on its "court," as the board of directors was then called.

A Jewish doctor in the tiny town of Williamsburg may be thought quite an oddity. How did Sequeyra happen to come, and what was his role in the town? Several scholars have researched Sequeyra, among them Norman Dain, in his book *Disordered Minds*, written for Colonial Williamsburg. Sequeyra was clearly ahead of most doctors of his day, concentrating more on medicines and drugs than on the medieval bloodletting practiced by most of his contemporaries.

The clearest indication of Sequeyra's acceptance is that he was called to the Governor's Palace in 1770 to attend Lord Botetourt. Sequeyra diagnosed Botetourt as having bilious fever and erysipelas, as we would call his ailments now. "His blood being in a bad condition," Sequeyra wrote, "it turned of the Malignant kind, having large Spots of a purple Colour upon his Breast and part of his back."

The 64-year-old royal governor "became delirious and had very strong convulsions for some time before he died," Sequeyra recorded. He was given a state funeral at Bruton Parish Church and buried beneath the William and Mary chapel.

Throughout the eighteenth century, Williamsburg usually had one or two resident doctors at any one time. Medical problems had increased after 1773, when the Publick Hospital for the insane was erected on Francis Street—the first of its kind in the colonies. Sequeyra was retained that year as the first visiting or part-time physician at the hospital, being paid 50 English pounds a year.

When Sequeyra was born in London in 1712, the most advanced medical school in Europe was at the University of Leiden in the Netherlands. So Sequeyra, who came of a prominent medical family, was sent there to study with a clinician named Hermann Boerhaave. He studied three years for his medical degree and

Winterthur

Dr. John de Sequeyra served the mental hospital from 1745 till he died in 1795.

remained in the Netherlands for a fourth year, getting further experience.

In 1745 Sequeyra sailed from England to Williamsburg to practice. Apparently he encountered no serious religious antagonism in Virginia. Like other adult whites in colonial Virginia, he was required to pay a tithe and a property tax to support the government and its established church. Some Jews in the colonies in those early years worshipped as Anglicans.

Susan Pryor, a Colonial Williamsburg interpreter who has also recently researched Sequeyra's life, found that he owned two adult slaves, two horses, and one or more horse-drawn conveyances. In 1772 he leased as his home a residence on Duke of Gloucester Street, now restored and a part of Shields Tavern, but obviously he never became rich.

One of Sequeyra's patients was Patsy Custis,

the epileptic daughter of Martha Dandridge Custis. Patsy, who spent part of her life at the Custis family's Williamsburg townhouse, died of the ailment in 1773.

Thomas Jefferson once wrote that Sequeyra introduced the tomato as an edible vegetable into Williamsburg and credited him with "being a great believer in the therapeutic value of the admirable vegetable." Sequeyra himself even believed that "A person who should eat a sufficient abundance of [tomatoes] would never die."

Sequeyra kept a revealing annual record of Williamsburg's ailments, which tells us much about early Virginians. He also wrote down his recommended treatments and left an indication of the survival rate for each disease. Most of the ailments are unidentifiable today.

Insanity was badly misunderstood in colonial times. Yet the creation in 1773 of Virginia's "Lunatick Asylum" was at least the start of public care for the mentally ill. Today Virginia has many governmental psychiatric clinics, plus three large state mental hospitals—one at Williamsburg (grown from the 1773 start) and the others at Petersburg and in southwest Virginia.

People don't like to talk about insanity, even now. The brick "Maison des foux"—as it is identified on the famous Frenchman's Map of 1781—on Francis Street has been avoided by people from the beginning. But it loomed large in the town's affairs from the eighteenth century until Eastern State Hospital (as it is currently named) was moved in the 1950s to Dunbar Farm, west of Williamsburg. It was second in payroll only to the college.

To observe the completion of the reconstructed 1773 hospital, Colonial Williamsburg published a scholarly booklet, "Quest for a Cure: The Public Hospital in Williamsburg, 1773-1885." It's a grim story. Twice major fires hit the asylum, killing two patients and destroying valuable equipment. Legislatures ignored and short-changed the asylum. In its first years, it was run like a jail or place of exile. Early knowledge of lunacy was more superstitious than scientific, resulting in cruel

Colonial Williamsburg

Virginia's mental hospital, built in 1773 and now reconstructed, was nation's first.

"cures." Families tried to forget about their "looney" relatives in Williamsburg.

The Public Hospital was conceived in the years 1770 to 1773 in a burst of enlightenment. Governor Francis Fauquier, who proposed it, was a benevolent and scientific man who had been a director of London's Foundling Hospital. The original building in Williamsburg was artfully designed by one of the 13 colonies' top architects, Robert Smith, who had designed Nassau Hall at Princeton and Carpenters Hall in Philadelphia. The reconstructed hospital contains two of the original 24 patient cells. Wooden-walled patient exercise yards were added in 1790, and have been reconstructed.

The first "keeper" of 1773 (a layman, as were all his successors until 1841) was James Galt, who had been keeper of the Public Gaol in Williamsburg. The Galt family dominated the asylum's control for most years from 1773 until 1862, when Dr. John Minson Galt, the last of four Galts to head it—died a few days after McClellan's federal troops entered Williamsburg in the Civil War and seized the asylum, along with the rest of the town. Dr. Galt's death was apparently of natural causes, but some suspect suicide.

For most of the nineteenth century, the asylum was a pawn in Virginia's politics. Whichever party controlled the General Assembly—

Colonial Williamsburg

William Trebell Galt was the asylum's keeper in 1800–1826, succeeding his father.

Whigs, Democrats, or Republicans—chose the keeper or superintendent. In 1852, for example, a fight between Whigs and Democrats disrupted its affairs for months, with dire effects on staff and patients.

In 1876, a bad fire destroyed one of the asylum's major buildings, and resulted in accusations and staff changes. Again, in 1885, fire struck the sleepy institution. Nearly 450 patients were evacuated in the night, with the loss of two. Destroyed was the beautiful building erected in 1773, which, in the interim, had had a third story and four Doric columns added.

Williamsburg had always been vulnerable to fires, and the asylum disaster of 1885 was one of the worst. The superintendent then, Dr. James Moncure, had been writing letters late on Saturday night, June 7, in his asylum office when his newly-installed electric light flared up. Forty-five minutes later he heard a patient screaming. Then came the cry, "Fire!"

Moncure realized that Williamsburg's fire equipment was unequal to the job and fired off a telegram to the Richmond fire department:

COME AT ONCE AND BRING ENGINE. EASTERN LUNATIC ASYLUM ON FIRE. WILL BE DESTROYED IF HELP IS NOT COMING SOON.

It took two hours and 40 minutes for Richmond's volunteer firemen to load a big fire engine on a C & O flat car and set out for Williamsburg. Understandably, the Public Hospital was gone when they reached it.

After that the building's foundations were covered over with dirt until Williamsburg archaeologists began unearthing them for study in 1971. The reconstructed hospital is built over them.

Many people can remember the iron-railed Eastern State Hospital grounds before the institution moved to Dunbar. A low brick building stood at the center, with tall grey plastered dormitories for inmates surrounding it. At that time Eastern State had more than 2,000 patients, and seemed increasingly incongruous next door to the Restoration.

It adds to the luster of Williamsburg's enlightened colonial leaders that they saw need for the first public mental hospital in the colonies. We've learned a lot about the mind since 1773, although it still seems hard to run a good psychiatric hospital.

13. *When Ben Franklin Visited*

YOU don't think of Benjamin Franklin as being on the Williamsburg scene, but the Pennsylvanian twice visited Virginia's colonial capital. He spent a month in Williamsburg in 1756 to organize a postal service in the colonies, and he stayed long enough to visit Hampton and Norfolk and to receive the first honorary degree given by the College of William and Mary. He was in Williamsburg briefly in 1763.

Old Ben became a friend of William Hunter, publisher of the *Virginia Gazette,* which was Virginia's only paper. It remained so until Hunter died in 1761. Together, the two chose postal routes connecting the 13 colonies and arranged for riders to carry the mail.

As publishers in two of Britain's major colonies, Franklin and Hunter had been appointed by the British government in 1753 as deputy postmasters for North America. In those days, newspaper offices served as post offices, with horsemen carrying mail in saddlebags from one town to the next.

Some light is shed on Franklin's 1756 visit by Wayne Barrett, editor of *Colonial Williamsburg,* a journal published by the Colonial Williamsburg Foundation. Barrett reports on

Franklin's Williamsburg connection in the Autumn 1988 issue, which also contains an extended article on colonial printers.

Franklin was 50 when he visited Williamsburg, but already he was famous for his *Pennsylvania Gazette*, his *Poor Richard's Almanac*, his experiments and inventions, and his presidency of the College and Academy of Pennsylvania—now the University of Pennsylvania.

Franklin reached Virginia by ship—stopping first at Hampton to visit John Hunter, a kinsman of William Hunter. He reached Williamsburg on March 24, writing his wife that he rejoiced to "find myself in the midst of Spring; Peaches on the Trees as big as Kidney Beans, and Asparagus on the Tables." He added that he and Hunter were "daily employ'd in settling our affairs. About the end of the week we are to take a tour into the country. Virginia is a pleasant country, now in full Spring; the People extremely obliging and polite."

On April 10 the mayor of Norfolk gave Franklin a document making him a "Burgess and Freeman of this Borough." President Thomas Dawson and the six masters of William and Mary also gave him an honorary master of arts degree, as Harvard and Yale had done earlier. The certificate is dated April 2, 1756, but the *Pennsylvania Gazette* reported that the ceremony took place April 20.

We are indebted to Franklin for a revealing anecdote about London attitudes toward the colonies. He wrote later that when the Reverend James Blair went from Virginia to London in 1691 to propose a college for the sake of Virginians' souls, one crusty courtier had exploded. "Souls? Damn their souls! Let them make tobacco!" Presumably Franklin heard it in Williamsburg.

Franklin also had an interest in a small paper mill which William Parks, Williamsburg's first printer, had set up in 1742 on Paper Mill Creek near the town.

Postal service in the 13 colonies slowly spread during the regime of Franklin and Hunter. Although England had established domestic postal service in 1657, it was years reaching the American colonies. Until then, mail had to be entrusted to ship captains and wagoners, who carried it as a favor or for a fee. The first part-time post offices in America were created by Parliament in 1710, and the mail was carried over a network of "post roads" stretching from New England south to Augusta, then capital of Georgia.

When Williamsburg printer William Hunter died, still a young man in 1761, his friend Franklin assumed responsibility for Hunter's son Billy.

Franklin's second trip to Williamsburg, in 1763, was briefer and less exciting. He wrote in Philadelphia on April 14, 1763, "I am just setting out on a Journey to Virginia, to settle accounts from the Executors of my late Colleague Mr. Hunter, and recover the money due from them to the General Post Office." These long-ago events are recalled in Williamsburg's Printing Office on Duke of Gloucester Street, where Virginia's first newspaper originated in 1736. Did Ben Franklin hang out there on his Virginia visits? Among those "extremely obliging and polite" people he met, were there such later Virginia revolutionaries as George Wythe, Peyton Randolph, and John Blair II whom he was to know after 1776 in Philadelphia?

I'm afraid we'll never know.

Benjamin Franklin in 1763 received an honorary degree from William and Mary.

William and Mary

14. *Botetourt, the Beloved*

ONE of the most talked-about people in Williamsburg is the nobly born Norborne Berkeley of England, who inherited the title "Baron de Botetourt." He was Virginia's next-to-last royal governor, serving from 1768 until his death in the Governor's Palace in 1770.

Botetourt was the best-loved governor in Virginia's 169 colonial years. His statue was even erected in the Capitol after he died. The reason he's talked about so much is that the Governor's Palace has recently been refurnished to look as it did when His Lordship lived there. Up till then, it had been furnished with a mixture of eighteenth-century antiques. Now Botetourt's taste totally prevails.

It's simpler now, and some say it tells you more. The beautiful walnut-paneled foyer of the Palace is full of muskets, mounted in geometric designs. Kitchens and pantries are filled with countless old household gadgets. Everything shown is something that was listed in a 16,500-item inventory which His Lordship's secretary-butler, William Marshman, made in Williamsburg after Botetourt died.

Botetourt was a classic embodiment of British imperialism at its most colorful. In his two years in Williamsburg, he had the feisty Virginians eating out of his hand. If he could have lived on to govern in 1775, instead of the bumbling Dunmore, things in Virginia might have been different.

Botetourt's charisma shines through his possessions. He had been a favorite of King George III, a society darling, and a groom of the Royal Bedchamber. Had it not been for the loss of his fortune when he was 50, he never would have exiled himself from the court of George III and come to this remote colony. It's sad to die in a strange country, with no family around you.

Historians once speculated on these things. Then, 26 years ago, an English historian named Bryan Little investigated Botetourt's life story in Bristol and Gloucestershire, where he had lived. Little found that the nobleman was nearly wiped out when copper deposits of Cornwall reached exhaustion in the 1760s—an event dramatized in the BBC television series, "Poldark." Botetourt's metal firm went bankrupt, and he was beset by irate creditors.

His friend King George III saved him by appointing him to succeed Lord Jeffrey Amherst, the non-resident governor of Virginia.

(Lieutenant Governor Francis Fauquier had actually governed in place of Amherst.) A London paper, the *Chronicle*, berated the king's appointment with this jingle:

Then thus unto a Scribe he spoke,
(A man at top o' th' trade)
"Lord Bow-at-Court has served me well,
'Tis fit he should be paid."

Diarist Horace Walpole saw Botetourt just before he sailed for Virginia in 1768 and wrote that he was "like patience on a monument, smiling in grief. He is totally ruined." Beneath the governor's benignity, Walpole saw Botetourt as a calculating implement of George III's will. "To Virginia he cannot be indifferent," Walpole confided. "He must turn their heads somehow or other. If his graces do not captivate them, he will enrage them to fury. I take all his douceur to be enamelled on iron."

History had recorded Botetourt as a bachelor, but Burke Davis has found that he had briefly married a Miss Christie and fathered a son. The ceremony was annulled by the English courts because it was performed in the Roman Catholic church.

Virginians of 1768 were flattered to learn in advance that popular Lieutenant Governor Fauquier was to be followed by a real-live nobleman—a friend of the king's. The *Virginia Gazette,* a few weeks later in October 1768, reported Botetourt's arrival at Hampton:

Last Tuesday evening arrived in Hampton Road, in eight weeks from Portsmouth, the *Rippon*, man-of-war, of 60 guns, Samuel Thompson, Esq., commander, having on board His Excellency the Right Hon. Norborne Baron de Botetourt, his majesty's Lieutenant and Governor General of this Colony and Dominion. Next morning his Excellency landed at Little England, and was saluted with a discharge of the cannon there.

Then the *Gazette* went on to tell:

His Excellency set out about noon for this

city [Williamsburg], where he arrived about sunset. His Excellency stopped at the Capitol, and was received at the gate by his Majesty's Council, the Hon. the Speaker [Peyton Randolph], the Attorney-General [John Randolph], the Treasurer [Robert Carter Nicholas], and many other gentlemen of distinction.

The account concluded:

Immediately upon His Excellency's arrival, the city was illuminated, and all ranks of people vied with each other in testifying their gratitude and joy that a Nobleman of such distinguished merit and abilities is appointed to preside over and live among them.

The next week's issue of the *Virginia Gazette* contained a well-written set of verses, designed to be sung by soloists and chorus. They began:

Virginia, see thy Governor appears;
The peaceful olive on his brow he wears.
Sound the shrill trumpets, beat the rattling drums;
From Great Britannia's isle his Lordship comes.

Another stanza describes Botetourt's arrival thus:

The Lordly prize th' Atlantic waves resign,
And now, Virginia, now the blessing's thine;
His listening ears will to your trust attend,
And be your Guardian, Governor, and Friend.

As Walpole had predicted, Botetourt invoked all the majesty of royal style to dignify his office in Virginians' eyes. That remains standard procedure today for Queen Elizabeth's viceroys, and it wows the commoners.

It is good to be able to report that, after such fulsome expectations, Botetourt was a success. Despite Walpole's innuendoes, he genuinely tried to help Virginia's colonists and to moderate Britain's policies. He faithfully attended prayers each morning at William and Mary, and he repeatedly assured Virginians that the interests of Virginia and Britain were identical.

"Consider well, and follow exactly, without passion or prejudice," he said, "the real interests of those you have the honor to represent. They are most certainly consistent with the prosperity of Great Britain."

Among his admirers was Thomas Jefferson, a young burgess from Albemarle, who responded to Botetourt's opening address to the General Assembly with the hope that "providence and the royal pleasure may long continue His Lordship the happy ruler of a free and happy people."

Alas, that was not long to be. In two years, the benign, soft-spoken governor died at the Palace of a lingering illness. He was buried at William and Mary after the grandest, most picturesque funeral that Williamsburg has ever seen from that day to this.

To show its admiration, the Assembly had a marble statue of Botetourt sculpted in London to stand in the Capitol. It survives today, blemished but imposing, in Swem Library at the college. It is a miracle that it lasted through the Revolution, when Americans destroyed most British monuments.

Botetourt's story has been restudied by Colonial Williamsburg recently for the Palace refurbishing. To examine His Lordship's papers and Palace records, Curator Graham Hood visited Botetourt's house, Stoke Park, at Gloucestershire in England. There and in the Gloucestershire Record Office he found many reminders of Virginia's colonial governor.

But the chief prize that Hood uncovered was the final draft of the 1770 inventory of Botetourt's furnishings in the Governor's Palace. It had been filed away by the late dowager Queen Mary, the mother of King George VI, Hood explains, while she was being sequestered during World War II bombings at Badminton, an English country house which contains some of the Botetourt records. There the Dowager Queen read through the inventory of Botetourt's Palace furnishings in Williamsburg and placed it in a package which she labelled "Interesting things." Thus obscured, it almost escaped Graham Hood's notice.

Lord Botetourt was the next-to-last of all British governors to occupy the Palace in Williamsburg.

Colonial Williamsburg

15. *Dunmore and Revolution*

THE seventeenth- and eighteenth-century British colonies in the New World were all governed by officials sent by the crown to lead them. Often two colonies were served in succession by the same royal governor.

That was the case with Virginia and the Bahamas, which had the misfortune to draw one of the worst governors. He was John Murray, the fourth Lord Dunmore, who was expelled from Virginia in the American Revolution and turned up as governor of the Bahamas 11 years later.

I discovered His Lordship when my guide in Nassau pointed out three strongly built eighteenth-century forts which Dunmore had erected in the 1790s against the threat of French invasion. (It was then rather a remote threat, but Dunmore liked building things.) Dunmore named the most elaborate of the three Fort Charlotte, in honor of his wife. He named another Fort Fincastle for his son, who bore the cadet title of Lord Fincastle. The third is Fort Montagu.

I wasn't surprised to learn that the obtuse Dunmore left as bad a record in the Bahamas in his 1787–96 tenure as he had in Virginia in 1771–1775. He had won the Bahamian appointment through the influence of his brother-in-law, Lord Stafford, who was a favorite of King George III—the British monarch during the long years from 1760 till 1820. But in Nassau, capital of the Bahamas, Dunmore showed the same miserable judgment as he had shown in Williamsburg. As a result, he was dismissed by the king in 1796 and ordered home to England in disgrace.

As Professor John Selby of the College of William and Mary has written of Dunmore's Bahamas days, "His style was as freewheeling and pugnacious [as in his Virginia governorship]. There were the same displays of temper. Once he allegedly caned a man in the street 'without the slightest provocation.'"

No, Dunmore proved as much a dud in the Bahamas as he had been in Virginia. After Dunmore was forced to leave Williamsburg in 1775 for having taken gunpowder at night from the colony's powder magazine, he sought safety aboard a British man-of-war. From its decks he sought to rally Virginians to resist the Revolution, collecting a handful of Virginia tories and a few slaves who responded to his offer of freedom if they would leave their masters.

John IV Earl of Dunmore
Captain in Regiment of Foot Guards
1745. Governor of Virginia 1770.

National Portrait Gallery of Scotland

Lord Dunmore fled Williamsburg in the Revolution and later was governor of the Bahamas.

But after a few discouraging exchanges with incensed Virginians at Norfolk and at Gwynn's Island, Dunmore sailed back to England with his family. After seeking and receiving extensive funds from George III's government for household goods and lands he left behind in Virginia, he got himself named governor of the Bahamas and went there in 1787.

It wasn't long before the Scotsman appointed his son Alexander collector of customs for Turks Island and then tried to name him lieutenant governor. He lived in the high style he'd enjoyed in Williamsburg's Governor's Palace. He expanded and redecorated Nassau's Government House, building a summer home called The Hermitage and holding lavish celebrations.

One of them, honoring George III, was described as "an elegant entertainment . . . at the Government House and in the evening . . . the most splendid illumination ever seen."

As in Virginia, Dunmore built forts too big for his troops to man. They nearly bankrupted the colony, and his government was charged with corruption. Then he denied that the legislature had any voice in the matter and refused to recognize a constitutional requirement that he call for general elections at least every seventh year, as in Great Britain.

On both matters, the Bahamas legislature passed resolutions protesting that Dunmore had treated it with "disrespect." As he had done in Williamsburg, Lord Dunmore in Nassau also plunged into money-making schemes which offended his constituents. He registered for many of the lots offered to American loyalists who had fled the 13 colonies in the Revolution. He also benefited from the Bahamas' first planned development, Dunmore Town, which he laid out.

By 1791 Bahamian complaints against Dunmore burst out in a confrontation. It had been nearly seven years since the high-handed Scotsman had called for a legislative election. People clamored for an audit of public accounts. In 1791 Dunmore had to prorogue, or close, the Bahamian assembly without appropriating public funds because assemblymen insisted on linking that with the appointment of commissioners of accounts.

From then on, protests against Lord Dunmore began to undermine him with London's Privy Council. After his patron, the Marquis of Stafford, left the British cabinet, Dunmore's days were numbered. In July 1796 he was dismissed as governor of the Bahamas and ordered home to England to explain his acts. For awhile, His Majesty's government seemed unwilling to finish paying for Dunmore's forts —Charlotte, Fincastle, and Montagu.

In the end, the government gave in to Dunmore's arguments. It gave the old troublemaker a 600-pound yearly pension. He and Lady Dunmore retired to Ramsgate, a seacoast resort in England, where he died in 1809.

When I stood on Nassau's shore and gazed up at Government House, I thought of the struggles in both Virginia and the Bahamas that preceded democratic government. Perhaps Dunmore, through his tyrannies, helped both Virginia and the Bahamas to grow up politically.

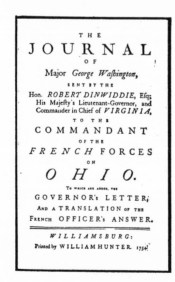

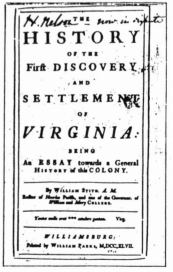

Colonial Williamsburg

Early Williamsburg publications reflect Virginia's pre-Revolutionary growth.

16. *A Patriot and a Tory*

OF all the human interest stories to emerge from Williamsburg over the centuries, the contrasting fates of Peyton Randolph and his brother John strike me as the most poignant. Peyton was a powerful lawyer and the most popular figure in Virginia until his death in 1775. John was his younger brother by six or seven years, also a lawyer, and also powerful as attorney general of Virginia.

The pathos lies in the fact that while Peyton became a leading spokesman for the Revolution, his brother John chose to remain loyal to England and went down in history as "John Randolph the Tory."

A final note of poignancy lies in the fact that John Randolph's son Edmund, also a lawyer, was an ardent patriot who, unlike his father, stayed in Virginia to fight in the Revolution and later to be U. S. attorney general and secretary of state under George Washington. He shared the views of his admired uncle Peyton rather than of his father.

The Randolph scenario has fascinated historians, but few papers survive to flesh out the contrasting men. We know that Peyton was large, commanding, and died of a stroke in Philadelphia after overtaxing himself in the patriot cause. John was thinner, more artistic, and had less taste for politics than Peyton. He played the violin, was an amateur architect, and a gardener.

The two brothers grew up in the house of their parents, Sir John and Lady Randolph, now exhibited by Colonial Williamsburg as the Peyton Randolph House. Sir John was the foremost lawyer of the 1720s and '30s, knighted by the king for service to the crown. He was a brother of a half dozen other leading Randolphs of Tidewater and the son of William and Mary Randolph of Turkey Island. Someone dubbed them "the Adam and Eve of Virginia society."

There's no evidence that Peyton and John didn't get along with each other. Each was a bright, well-educated, public man. They were both friends of their cousin, Thomas Jefferson, who wrote admiringly of Peyton. Both moved in the colony's top social circle, made up of the governor, members of his council, and leading planters, lawyers, clergymen, and a doctor or two.

Says a Colonial Williamsburg study, "In private life [John Randolph] was especially attractive and retained the friendship of many of the

Revolutionary patriots, who enjoyed his company and respected his intellectual attainments and personal integrity. His Williamsburg home was a popular literary and social center."

John lived in maturity on what is now South England Street, building a house on land he inherited from his father. Known in the nineteenth century as Tazewell Hall, his house was moved about 1908 and later dismantled and sold to Lewis McMurran in Newport News.

John Randolph not only experimented with gardening, but wrote *A Treatise on Gardening by a Citizen of Virginia.* The work was the first of its sort in the colonies. No copy survives.

As the clouds of war gathered in 1775, John Randolph must have been a troubled man. He loved the England of his forefathers, for he had studied law at the Inns of Court there, like his father and his brother Peyton before him. Yet Peyton was in 1775 president of the Continental Congress that was actively considering revolt.

Colonial Williamsburg

Peyton Randolph was a Revolutionist, but his brother John was a tory.

Colonial Williamsburg

Sir John Randolph was father of Williamsburg's prominent political leaders.

In August of 1775, while Peyton lay ill in Richmond on his way to preside over the Congress in Philadelphia, John Randolph in Williamsburg wrote to his son Edmund, who had volunteered for military service. The distressed tory father declared:

My dear Edmund:

I wrote you a long letter . . . why I thought your military undertaking will not suit your situation or be so advantageous to you as residing in Williamsburg. Your uncle [Peyton] we hear is dangerously ill at Richmond. . . . It is thought his duration here will be but short. You should never be out of the way, when so much depends on your presence.

I shall certainly go to England with my family before October. I want you very much to take my place at the capitol. His majesty will provide for me a home [in England] and you may certainly get into my office. I propose selling all my estate both real and personal at the next meeting [of the General Assembly] in October. . . . I have appointed yourself and Uncle Peyton my trustees for selling my estate and shall join Mr. [John] Blair with you.

Consider what an honorable and advantageous outset you will make in the law. Is not the glory of the Cabinet equal to the [battle] field? Is not this better than broken limbs, fatigue, shattered health, and an eternal want of money? For God's sake return to your family and indeed to yourself. Abandon not your sisters, who are wretched about you. Come back and heaven will prosper all your undertakings.

Peyton in fact recovered and proceded to Philadelphia. John Randolph meantime took his wife and daughters to Norfolk September 8, 1775, and sailed for England. Colonial Williamsburg's film *The Story of a Patriot,* depicts him telling a younger Virginian, "I am going home," just before he left Williamsburg. In the absence of his son and brother, he appointed John Blair and James Cocke—both patriots—to receive funds due to him and to pay off his debts.

Six weeks after John sailed for England, Peyton became ill again at dinner in Philadelphia and there died at 54 of a stroke. The Continental Congress attended a state funeral in Philadelphia's Christ Church and Randolph's remains were buried there till they could be moved to Virginia. An interment service was held at the college chapel where Randolph's casket was sealed with ceremony. His nephew, Edmund, had accompanied the casket from Philadelphia.

Although he had no children, Williamsburg's *Virginia Gazette* on November 29, 1776, described the dead Peyton as "a father, an able counsellor, and one of [our] firmest patriots."

As for John Randolph the Tory, he spent the Revolutionary years in England, grieving for

Peyton Randolph house on Courthouse Green is open to today's visitors.

Colonial Williamsburg

his son and his friends. Because of the war, it was difficult for him to get funds from Virginia. His last years were fraught with problems.

After John died in England in 1784, his daughter Ariana and her husband John Wormeley—also a Virginia tory refugee—brought his body back to Williamsburg, as he had requested. John was buried in the college chapel beside his father and brother, both distinguished alumni, like him.

For years after the Revolution, American patriots excoriated the memory of John Randolph the Tory, but times have changed. The years have softened bitterness toward him, whose worst sin was his loyalty to the England that had educated and prospered him.

As for Peyton, he was immortalized by Thomas Jefferson in an oft-quoted tribute. "He was indeed a most excellent man," Jefferson wrote, "and one who was ever more beloved and respected by his friends." Had he lived, perhaps John's last years might have been happier.

Colonial Williamsburg

The President's House at William and Mary housed French officers in the Revolution.

17. *The Frenchman's Map*

AN English-born historian, Alan Simpson, has solved most of the mysteries surrounding the long-celebrated "Frenchman's Map" used by researchers in restoring Williamsburg in the 1920s and 1930s. Simpson, a former trustee of Colonial Williamsburg and an ex-president of Vassar College, was led to the quest by his curiosity about the hand-drawn map, found in the William and Mary library, and called "the bible of the Restoration." He has recorded his findings in *The Mysteries of the Frenchman's Map of Williamsburg, Virginia,* published by Colonial Williamsburg.

Simpson recounts that his quest began over a decade ago and led him through archives in France, various universities, and Williamsburg. The original map was drawn in pen and ink and color on paper $25^1/_2$ by $16^1/_2$ inches. It is titled in French, "Plan of the city and environs of Williamsburg in Virginia, America. March 11, 1782."

The map's existence was first reported, Simpson notes, in a letter from Dr. W. A. R. Goodwin to John D. Rockefeller on January 11, 1927. Goodwin, who had recently persuaded Rockefeller to partially restore the town, wrote "We have found an old map at the College of Williamsburg in 1782. This map locates every house in Williamsburg at that date. . . . This map will be invaluable in our study."

Simpson set out to answer six questions:
(1) When was the map done?
(2) Why was it done?
(3) How was it done?
(4) How was it used?
(5) Who was the author?
(6) How did the map get to William and Mary?

Uncertainty about the map's date was caused by the map's hand-scripted date, which looks more like "1786" than "1782." However, Simpson found that eighteenth-century French copybooks showed a variant "2" that looked like the digit "6." Simpson was convinced the 1782 date was correct, gathering from other evidence that it was made in Williamsburg that year as a billeting map for use of French officers under General Rochambeau. He cites a letter from Rochambeau indicating the cooperation of Williamsburg citizens in arranging for the French billeting. The French army of 7,000 men wintered in Williamsburg for eight months after the American-French victory at Yorktown on October 19, 1781.

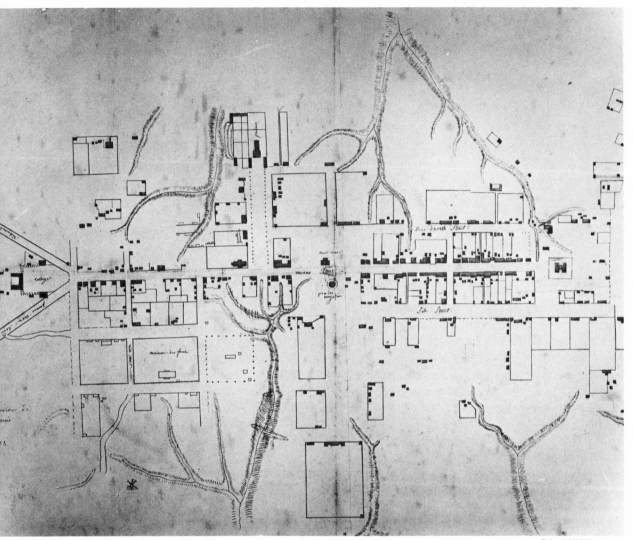

Colonial Williamsburg

The "Frenchman's Map" drawn in 1782, aided Williamsburg's restoration.

In answer to his third question, "How was it done?" Simpson concludes that the map was paced off by engineers. Since the horizontal scale of the map is longer than the vertical, he concludes that two men paced the map, with different strides and therefore two different scales.

Answering his fourth question, "How was it used?" Simpson concludes it enabled the French army's billeting master to show officers and enlisted men where they were to stay during the eight-month Williamsburg occupation.

Turning to the map's authorship, Simpson considers as possible draftsmen several well-known French engineers and cartographers among Rochambeau's officers. He mentions five of the best known, all Rochambeau quarter-masters. They were Victor Collot, Charles de

Beville, Mathieu Dumas, and the brothers Alexandre and Charles Berthier. However, he finds no conclusive evidence. He hopes "the identity of the unknown author . . . may some day be revealed."

Simpson made many efforts to learn what happened to the map between the time it was drawn and the time Goodwin brought it to Rockefeller's attention from the archives in the William and Mary library. He learned that a

Colonial Williamsburg

Historian Alan Simpson discovered some of the Frenchman's Map's secrets.

New York contractor, John D. Crimmins, whose hobby was old maps, was persuaded in 1909 by Betty Custis Ambler of Williamsburg to give the map to the librarian of William and Mary. The librarian, Emily Christian, later recalled that Crimmins had acquired the map from "someone who had taken it" in the Civil War, presumably a Union soldier.

The college's librarian when the Rockefeller Restoration began was Earl G. Swem, who refused to let the map be photographed. However, Swem finally agreed to let Bishop John Bentley of Hampton, an ex-student of the college, draw a penciled copy of the map for the guidance of Restoration researchers. Later Swem permitted photographs, and eventually the map was reproduced in facsimile for the Restoration by the Meriden Gravure Company of Connecticut.

Concluding his study, Simpson speculates on how the map was saved: "Perhaps the map was given to a local citizen—like St. George Tucker, who had fought at the siege, or like the barrack-master general—as a memento. . . . Perhaps it just lay quietly in some private library."

"All that we really know," he concludes of his treasure hunt, "is that it eventually surfaced within a few miles of where it had been drawn to tease the imagination of anyone who enjoys a good historical puzzle."

Simpson's booklet, illustrated with maps and pictures, is a popular seller in Williamsburg book shops. I recommend it for lovers of mystery stories.

18. *1782: Dawn of Peace*

THE year 1782 was an awkward one in Williamsburg. Americans and French forces had defeated Cornwallis at Yorktown the preceding October 19, but the British reaction to that defeat wouldn't be known till 1782, after ships had carried the news across the Atlantic. Would Britain quit or would the war go on? The mood was nervous when the year dawned, but before it ended, the word had come from London that Lord North, the wartime prime minister, had resigned and Britain wanted peace.

After Cornwallis's surrender at Yorktown, George Washington and Rochambeau moved to Williamsburg with their staffs. Washington entertained his officers and the French at dinners at Mrs. Campbell's Coffee House, running up astronomical bills in that day's currency. Then Washington and his army went north to receive the plaudits of the Continental Congress in Philadelphia.

General Rochambeau, the French commander, and his 7,000 French soldiers remained in Williamsburg until the following July before they, too, went to Philadelphia. After the British sued for an end to the war in late 1782, the French sailed home. Peace had come at last.

Most occupying armies are hated, but Rochambeau and his men were warmly admired in the little town of Williamsburg. General Rochambeau and his aides lived for eight months in the Wythe House, while other French officers were billeted in Raleigh Tavern and Williamsburg houses. Rochambeau's army meanwhile encamped in tents west of Williamsburg, near the present Eastern State Hospital. They were permitted to come to town only occasionally.

Meanwhile, the French used the President's House at William and Mary as a hospital for officers. American soldiers were hospitalized in the Governor's Palace, which had ceased to serve as such when Governor Jefferson moved Virginia's government to Richmond in April 1780.

In a series of mishaps, the President's House burned on the night of November 23, 1781, not long after the French had moved in, while the Governor's Palace burned a month later, December 22. Both housed ailing soldiers.

On January 15, 1782, Mayor William Holt and the corporation of the City of Williamsburg waited on Rochambeau at the Wythe House and presented him with an address of welcome.

Colonial Williamsburg

General Rochambeau and his French army spent the winter of 1781–82 in Williamsburg.

"We avail ourselves on this occasion," it read, "to remind you of the obligations which we have to your Excellence of the discipline and good order which were strictly observed by the troops quartered in this city and of the scrupulous attention to never violate the privileges and immunities of the free citizens."

Rochambeau was admired as a thoughtful, effective general. Washington liked him and his staff. They included such officers as the Chevalier Francois-Jean de Chastellux, the Bavarian Count Ludwig von Closen, and the aristocratic Duc de Broglie. They had a sort of officers' mess at Raleigh Tavern, where they hung out when not on duty.

George Washington wrote a letter on January 2, 1782, to de Broglie, congratulating him on the bravery of his young cousin, the Chevalier de la Meth, who had led the storming of Redoubt 9 during the Yorktown siege. "Your

brave young Kinsman will prove a most valuable Officer to his Country," Washington wrote, "and an ornament to the noble family to which he is allied."

De Chastellux later became famous as author of a book of American journeys called *Travels in North America*, published in Paris in 1786 and re-published in this country. Chastellux got Rochambeau's permission to leave the French army in Williamsburg in April for those travels. His first stop was with Jefferson at Monticello. "Mr. Jefferson is the first American who has consulted the Fine Arts to know how he should shelter himself from the weather," Chastellux wrote after that visit.

Baron von Closen especially enjoyed the female society of Williamsburg. He cut silhouettes of a dozen or so ladies of the town— various Blairs, Carys, Harrisons, Randolphs, Nelsons, and Carters. The Bavarian sent the silhouettes back home to his castle near

Colonial Williamsburg

The Chevalier de Chastellux began his book of American travels in Williamsburg.

Munich "to reveal the simplicity and oddity of Virginia ladies' hair-dos," he wrote.

In 1782, the College of William and Mary remained closed, as it had been since the British under Cornwallis had first come to the Peninsula. The college president and his wife, Bishop and Mrs. James Madison, had then sought refuge at Fincastle, only returning in May 1782. As the college was still occupied by the French, Madison rented the Archibald Blair House as his home temporarily.

After the Yorktown battle, Williamsburg lacked many necessities, but life was spirited. "Every article of living, corn except, is dear in this country," wrote American officer Peter Colt from Williamsburg that spring to his wife in Connecticut. "The difficulty is increased by a universal spirit of gambling, horse racing, [and] other expensive diversions."

Colt described Williamsburg's decline. "Its glory is departed," he wrote. "Were it not for the French officers it would be a dead calm. . . . When we depart the inhabitants may starve."

At the mental hospital in town, patients were on short rations. "If no relief can be had," Judge John Blair suggested, "it would be highly proper to take some measures for returning the poor wretches to their respective parishes."

During those early 1782 months, Williamsburg and the colonies remained in a state of war. Dispatch riders took messages from Rochambeau to George Washington in Philadel-

phia. Meanwhile, Admiral de Grasse's navy had gone to the Caribbean to continue the sea war against Britain. On February 12, 1782, de Grasse captured the British island of St. Kitts. However, he was soon defeated by a British fleet and was taken captive.

Then came good news. The House of Commons urged King George III to end the war with America. Under pressure, Prime Minister Lord North resigned. In Philadelphia, Virginia Delegate Theodorick Bland wrote to his kinsman St. George Tucker in Williamsburg an enthusiastic poem, "The Work is Done," which began:

Now War shall Cease
And Milk-eyed Peace
Shall bless our Happy land
Our Union Strong
Shall last as long
As we go hand in hand.

In June Rochambeau paid the college in full for fire damage to the President's House. Letters and papers from Britain arrived by ship at Yorktown confirming that Britain sought peace. Thomas Jefferson, grieving the death of his Martha at Monticello, was sent to Paris to negotiate terms. On July 1 Rochambeau bade farewell to Virginia and led his army northward to Philadelphia. They were on their way back to France.

Seldom does history record so happy an "occupation" as did Williamsburg in 1781–82.

19. *Williamsburg's Shocking Scandal*

OF all the figures in Williamsburg's historic past, the most romantic is Commodore Lewis L. Warrington, a hero of the War of 1812 who became Secretary of the Navy in 1844.

Why is Warrington romantic? Because he was the illegitimate son of a well-known French officer in the American Revolution who had a wartime romance with a Williamsburg girl in 1782. The affair has been little publicized because family letters describing it have never been published. But Warrington's paternity was known by Williamsburgers in his lifetime.

Here's the story as it emerges from Williamsburg and Yorktown records of the 1780s:

After Cornwallis surrendered at Yorktown on October 19, 1781, the American and French armies went into winter quarters. Washington led his troops north to Philadelphia to be near the Continental Congress, while General Rochambeau brought most of the French troops to Williamsburg, where they encamped from November 1781 until the following July. The rest of the French were billeted for those eight months in Hampton, Yorktown, and West Point.

Both the French and Americans were waiting to see if the British would end the war. Roch-

ambeau enjoined his officers and men in Williamsburg not to offend their Virginia hosts. To minimize the difficulties of fraternization, about half the French enlisted men were encamped east of town, near the empty Capitol. The other half had their tented village west of town, near the College of William and Mary.

Rochambeau himself occupied the Wythe House on Palace Green, and his chief staff officers were billeted as distinguished guests in the Raleigh Tavern and townhouses close by the Wythe House.

Rochambeau and several of his officers wrote accounts of their winter in Williamsburg. The general foxhunted frequently, mounted on a fine Virginia horse. Once he rode six miles out of town to examine a dam built by beavers. According to familiar legend, the courtly general addressed the students of William and Mary in Latin because his English was poor. He and his officers were honored guests at several Williamsburg banquets and balls.

Living that winter of 1782 in the Brush-Everard House on Palace Green was a Mrs. Susanna Riddell, the widow of a Yorktown physician. She had as her wards two young women from Yorktown, Camilla and Rachel

Warrington. On November 3, 1782, the unmarried Rachel gave birth in the Brush-Everard House to a boy whom she named Lewis Warrington—a scandalous illegitimate birth in Williamsburg's small circle.

Who was Lewis Warrington's father? The records of Williamsburg in 1782 do not say. However, several unpublished letters written by Rachel's friend, Elizabeth Ambler of Yorktown, name Joseph Rochambeau, 31, son of the French general and a junior quartermaster officer in the French army in Williamsburg. The letters remain in the ownership of an Ambler descendant in Richmond and have never been published, though I have seen them.

When and how did the Williamsburg girl meet the French officer? We know little except that Rachel Warrington was providing meals for ill soldiers during the Revolution. The State Auditor's papers for that period show 14 pounds and 19 shillings "paid Thomas Pate for Rachel Warrington board for Sick Soldiers." She may have met young Rochambeau when he was a hospital patient.

The illegitimate birth of Lewis Warrington was an incident common to wartime, when life is fleeting and passions run high. But the French officer apparently did not offer to marry Rachel and acknowledge his son. Instead, he left Rachel behind in Williamsburg when he sailed back to France.

Subsequent records of York County show

Colonial Williamsburg

Rachel Warrington gave birth to her son in the Brush-Everard House.

that Rachel Warrington, "spinster," in 1786 married one Richard Brown in York County when young Lewis was four years old. Fourteen years later Lewis was appointed a United States Navy midshipman. He had risen to lieutenant in the War of 1812 and was commanding the U. S. sloop Peacock when he met and defeated the British warship Epervier in a "sharp action" off the Florida coast. He became an American war hero, receiving a gold medal from Congress and a sword from the Commonwealth of Virginia. He followed this with other victories, becoming a commodore, then the Navy's top rank.

Warrington's exploits evidently reached Europe. When his father learned of his bravery, he wrote his son and offered to acknowledge him and give Warrington his name, a proud one in France, according to a family contemporary. However, "the Commodore indignantly recalled these tardy overtures," the record says.

History does not record the further fate of Rachel Warrington Brown, but we know that Lewis's father became a well-known officer. He led French forces in quelling a Negro revolt in the French colony of Haiti in 1793, languished for a while as British prisoner-of-war in England, and died in battle in 1813, when England and her allies defeated Napoleon's army at Leipzig in the so-called "Battle of the Nations."

As for Commodore Lewis Warrington, he died peacefully while still in naval service in 1851, the second oldest officer in the Navy at

U.S. Naval Academy

Commodore Lewis Warrington, USN, was the illegitimate grandson of General Rochambeau.

that time. His portrait, by Rembrandt Peale, is often reproduced.

Such is the story of Williamsburg's most mysterious celebrity, a grandson of the famous General Rochambeau. It is only one of many secrets to be found in early records of Williamsburg and Yorktown.

Gift of Colonel and Mrs. Edgar Garbisch,
Virginia Museum of Fine Arts

George Washington presided at the 1787 Constitutional Convention in Philadelphia.

20. *Writing the Constitution*

THOUGH seven men went north from Virginia to the Constitutional Convention in Philadelphia in 1787, only three of them signed the document.

Furthermore, one of the seven—George Mason of Gunston Hall—didn't like the Constitution and opposed Virginia's ratification of it in a state convention, held at Richmond in 1788. There Mason and Patrick Henry led an attack on the "centralizing" document that nearly led Virginia to repudiate it. The vote for approval was 89 for and 79 against. Only the persistence of James Madison and the prestige of George Washington enabled Virginia to vote "yes" for union.

Of the 13 states, Virginia was the most divided. Yet it was crucial to the five-month Philadelphia debates because Virginia was the most populous, largest, and oldest of the 13. It heavily influenced the "Southern Tier" states of Maryland, the Carolinas, and Georgia.

When delegates had met in Philadelphia in May 1787, they unanimously chose Washington to preside. But not even the famous general could influence Virginia delegates Mason and Edmund Randolph to give the Constitution their approval. Randolph later changed his mind and supported it in the Virginia ratifying convention.

Two other delegates—George Wythe of Williamsburg and Dr. James McClurg of Richmond—also didn't sign for Virginia. Wythe was called away by his wife's illness. McClurg had business that kept him away.

Patrick Henry, who had grown conservative in old age, voiced the anti-Constitution sentiments of many rural, slave-owning Virginians. He declined to be a delegate to Philadelphia because he "smelled a rat." Henry later thought the Constitution inadequately protected the states' rights of the slave-holding South. His fears crystallized 74 years later in the Civil War.

The Constitution was partly a Virginian achievement. Its champion was small, 36-year-old Madison, whose "Virginia plan" was largely adopted. Washington was its most influential advocate and signed for Virginia with Madison. The third Virginia signer was John Blair II of Williamsburg, great-nephew of James Blair who founded William and Mary College.

Of all Virginia localities, Williamsburg had the largest hand in the Constitution. John Blair and Wythe both lived here in 1787, while Randolph and McClurg had recently moved from Williamsburg to Richmond, Virginia's new capital.

Williamsburg's delegates were a distinguished group. Wythe, lawyer and professor, was the only one of Virginia's delegates who had signed the Declaration of Independence in 1776. Blair was a judge, whom Washington would name to the Supreme Court. Randolph was the son of John Randolph "the Tory," who

Colonial Williamsburg

George Wythe was prevented by his wife's illness from signing the Constitution.

had returned to England in 1775 rather than revolt. And McClurg, born in Hampton, had taught medicine at William and Mary from 1779 until about 1784.

Madison made by far the biggest Constitutional contribution. He based his concepts of federal-state relations and of balanced executive-legislative-judicial powers on classical and British precedents. But little, quiet-spoken Madison was a poor speaker, so Virginia's governor, delegate Edmund Randolph, 34, present-ed Madison's plans. Today Madison's hand-written records of the debates in the Library of Congress are the best inside account of that "Miracle at Philadelphia." He tried to balance advantages between big states and small, North and South, farmers and merchants. That's why he's called "father of the Constitution."

Some debates pitted Mason, 62 and brilliant, against Madison. Mason feared a powerful presidency and refused to accept Madison's compromises. Even so, some of his ideas went into the Constitution and its first 10 amendments, called the Bill of Rights, which Congress enacted in 1789. It was based on Mason's Virginia Declaration of Rights of 1776.

Thomas Jefferson wasn't at Philadelphia in 1787 because he was representing America in Paris. Another Virginia leader, Richard Henry Lee, opposed the union he saw coming and, like Patrick Henry, declined to be a delegate to Philadelphia.

Slavery was a hot issue at Philadelphia, for five of the 13 states were heavily slave-owning. A few enlightened Americans in 1787 were urging slavery's end. Some were giving money to repatriate blacks in Africa. Mason proposed to outlaw slavery in the Constitution, but Georgia and South Carolina objected. It took another 78 years to end human servitude in the United States.

Sectionalism flared also over Congress's right to regulate commerce. In Virginia, Henry feared Northern tariffs would protect Northern industry but sacrifice Southern farming. Many Revolutionary War veterans, however, favored the document because of Washington's belief that a central power was needed to deter foreign aggressors.

When Virginia's ratifying convention met, the eyes of the 13 colonies were on Richmond. Only eight states had thus far approved the Constitution, and nine were required to put it into effect. Washington declined to become a delegate, but he was actively trying to persuade other Virginians. He wrote one letter, frequently quoted, that read: "I am fully persuaded . . .

that [either the Constitution] or disunion is before us."

In approving the Constitution, Virginia attached an "escape clause" declaring that "powers granted under the Constitution, being derived from the people of the United States, may be resumed by them whensoever the same shall be perverted to their injury or oppressions, and . . . every power not granted thereby remains with them and at their will; that therefore no right of any denomination can be cancelled, abridged, restrained, or modified by the Congress." That was later cited as basis for Virginia's secession from the union in 1861.

Unfortunately, the debates on the Constitution estranged many Virginians. Mason and Washington, neighbors in Fairfax and once friends, ceased to see each other. Benjamin Harrison, a leading Revolutionist, was refused a federal appointment by President Washington. Their friendship cooled. The Constitution added greatly to the stature of Washington, Madison, and young John Marshall, who helped sell it to Virginia's ratifiers. He was named by President Adams in 1800 as secretary of state and in 1801 as chief justice.

Today, two centuries after the Constitution's birth, its provisions are alive and relatively unchanged. In most respects Madison's brainchild has proven a valid guide.

Will it be adequate for another 200 years? Time will tell.

William and Mary

James McClurg, an ex-Williamsburger, left the convention without signing.

21. *John Blair, Jr., Forgotten Man*

ONE of Williamsburg's least-known major figures was John Blair, Jr., who was appointed by President Washington to the U. S. Supreme Court in 1789—one of the first men to serve on the court. One historian has called Blair "Virginia's Forgotten Signer." He refers to Blair's signing of the Constitution, along with his fellow Virginia delegates George Washington and James Madison.

Well, who was John Blair, Jr.? His portrait shows a long-faced gentleman with a large nose and a balding thatch of reddish hair. The records reveal him as a rather colorless man, wedded to the law. His tombstone in Bruton Parish churchyard notes that he "was honored with a variety of the most important public appointments." It concludes that "he never excited enmity nor lost a Friend."

How come Blair is so little known? I believe it's because he was a less personable and versatile man than such Williamsburg contemporaries as Wythe, Peyton and John Randolph, and St. George Tucker. The once-important Blair family in Williamsburg died out with John Blair, Jr., but the line persisted in Virginia through the marriages of various Blair women to Peachy, Braxton, and Banister men. I came to know "forgotten" John Blair, Jr. when I wrote the biography, *James Blair of Virginia*, for the University of North Carolina Press.

James was the little-known Scottish cleric who emigrated to Virginia in 1685 and eight years later founded the College of William and Mary. James's brother, Dr. Archibald Blair, followed James from Scotland to Williamsburg in the 1690s as a physician. Archibald's son, John Blair, Sr. of Williamsburg, became president of the Governor's Council and also inherited the childless James's fortune.

It was the first John Blair's son, born in Williamsburg in 1732 (the same year as George Washington) whom we're concerned with here. He was John, junior.

John, Jr. attended William and Mary, studied law in London's Inns of Court, and married Jean Balfour of Hampton, daughter of a tobacco shipper. In 1766, John, Jr. was elected to the House of Burgesses. Twice he was Virginia's acting governor. Soon he became a judge of the General Court. After the Revolution he was named to Virginia's first Court of Appeals, now the Virginia Supreme Court.

Jefferson wrote Madison about this time to

Colonial Williamsburg painting
given by Margaret St. John,

*John Blair, Jr. of Williamsburg was one of three
Virginia signers of the Constitution.*

express "solicitude for drawing the first characters of the Union into the judiciary." He suggested "Mr. Blair and Colonel [Edmund] Pendleton as Associate and District Judges." Pendleton declined, but Blair accepted.

Blair knew George Washington well. The general had written Blair during the siege of Yorktown to request use of William and Mary buildings to hospitalize injured soldiers. As rector of the college's Board of Visitors, John Blair, Jr. granted Washington's request.

At the Constitutional Convention 1787, John Blair, Jr. was clearly overshadowed by big guns like Washington, Madison, Hamilton, Elbridge Gerry, and Benjamin Franklin. Madison's journal makes little mention of him. But Blair spoke out at least once, opposing a one-man presidency. Therein he sided with Edmund Randolph, who favored a triumvirate rather than a single executive, which Randolph called "the foetus of Monarchy."

When the time came to sign the Constitution, Randolph and George Mason declined, along with Gerry, because they felt it was drawn up "without the knowledge or idea of the people." But John Blair joined Washington and Madison to endorse the document—one of only 39 delegates to do so.

The Constitution faced an equally difficult hurdle when it was considered by Virginia's ratification convention. Of that gathering in Richmond, Washington wrote Lafayette, saying "Pendleton, Wythe, Blair, Madison . . . and many others of our first characters will be advocates for its adoption." Blair did not disappoint Washington. He voted for ratification.

Writes one Williamsburg historian, "Blair's loyalty did not go unrewarded." President Washington nominated him to the United States Supreme Court, passing over George Wythe, presumably because Wythe was 66—six years older than Blair. In any case, the Supreme Court was by no means the plum then that it is now. It required Blair to travel to New York, where the federal capital then was, and to ride a circuit to hear regional cases, as early Supreme Court justices did. John Marshall did so a few years later.

John Blair remained on the Supreme Court until 1796 when, 64 and ailing, he resigned and came home to live his last years. He died in Williamsburg in 1800, survived by several daughters but no sons.

A fellow Philadelphia Convention delegate called Blair "one of the most respectable men in Virginia, both on account of his family as well as fortune." He added that Blair's "good sense, and most excellent principles, compensate for other deficiencies."

In his will, John Blair requested "the humane treatment of my slaves" and warned his heirs of a condition in his will that would free his slaves if his inheriting children should disregard his instruction.

John Blair, Jr. was a man worth remembering.

22. *When the Music Stopped*

EW places in America have been described more extravagantly than Williamsburg. Nowadays the town is constantly visited by many writers, most of whom react enthusiastically. But it wasn't always so. Many early visitors didn't like it, chastising the town's "unhealthy" climate, its faded appearance and, until the Civil War, its many slaves, who outnumbered white people in town until well after blacks were emancipated.

One of the town's visiting critics was Jedidiah Morse, a New England cleric who came to Williamsburg in 1792 to gather material for his *American Universal Geography*, which was to be published in Boston. Morse (father of Samuel F. B. Morse, who invented the telegraph) wrote critically:

> Everything in Williamsburg appears dull, forsaken, and melancholy—no trade—no amusements, but the infamous one of gaming—no industry, and very little appearance of religion. The unprosperous state of the College, but principally the removal of the Seat of Government, have contributed much to the decline of this city.

That was too much for St. George Tucker, a Bermuda lawyer who had moved his family to Williamsburg after the Revolution. Tucker replied to Morse, writing in part:

> There are many very comfortable houses left, which, having undergone some repairs, contribute to vary the scene, and there are still some neat gardens and pleasant situations; it seems to be the idea of the inhabitants that Williamsburg has seen its worst day. They also have fish, crabs, oysters, wild fowl, and excellent butter, vegetables, and fruits. In short, how contemptible soever Williamsburg . . . might have appeared in the eyes of a traveller, few villages can boast a more pleasant situation, more respectable inhabitants, or a more agreeable and friendly society.

When Morse's geography appeared in 1805, it was a little more objective and factual. Morse acknowledged his reliance on Jefferson's recent *Notes on the State of Virginia*, (a very critical book) and regretted that "the disparity of fortunes and of intellectual acquirements is very great [in Virginia], and it is to be regretted that the mass of the people are unenlightened. Industry is not so general as to the northward of them; dissipation in various forms has been more prevalent in this state than perhaps in any other in the Union."

Much as I hate to admit it, Morse was largely right. Drinking, gambling, cockfighting, and horse racing had become general, especially among planters. In fact, the General Assembly by law forbade bets of more than $7, which had reduced horse racing in the Old Dominion and benefited sportsmen in Kentucky and Maryland.

Describing the decline of the College of William and Mary, Morse wrote that "the admission of the learners of Latin and Greek filled the college with children. This rendering it disagreeable and degrading to young gentlemen already prepared for entering on the science." The college was also poor and ill-attended, having lost British support.

Morse applauded a plan to create the first Virginia public schools. The plan called for the state to pay for educating able, poor boys; well-to-do parents would pay for their own sons. However, the proposal excluded blacks and most girls. Morse concluded that "This is ingenious but probably an impracticable theory." Not until after the Civil War did Virginia get public schools in all areas.

The New Englander found that Virginia's principal crops were tobacco, wheat, corn, pork, peas, beef, and brandy. Also important to the economy were river shipping, lumbering, naval stores, and trapping. Iron mining, fishing, and horse raising were smaller sources. Industry was almost nonexistent.

Virginia's population in the 1800 census was only 880,192 people, though the state was then the most populous in the nation. Of its people, 534,396 were white and 345,796 black. Norfolk was the largest town, with about 7,000 people. Elizabeth City County (now Hampton) had about 3,000, Warwick County (now Newport News) about 2,000, and the counties of York about 3,000, Gloucester about 8,000, Mathews about 6,000, and Isle of Wight about 9,000.

Morse wrote glowingly of Monticello, whose prospect was "charming." He found that Jefferson had 120 "workmen" (slaves) who made a ton of nails a day. He noted that Williamsburg had 1,400 people and 200 houses, many houses "going to decay." He visited the town's lunatic asylum and found it "neatly kept" but that "convalescents have not sufficient room for free air and exercise."

Unpleasant as it was for Virginians to be judged thus by a New England Congregationalist, a few sober Southerners already realized the state was declining, chiefly because of slavery. Education and industry were barely taking root. But regional tempers became inflamed, and the Civil War was the dreadful consequence. Had Jefferson and antislavery Virginians had their way, the Old Dominion might have abolished slavery in the early years of the republic and perhaps have averted civil war.

Williamsburg should have paid more heed to the criticisms of the Rev. Jedidiah Morse.

Removal of the capital to Richmond in 1780 left the college the main activity of Williamsburg.

College of William and Mary

Virginia Historical Society

A well cleaner plied his trade at the end of the nineteenth century in Williamsburg.

II.
Years of Trial and Decline

1787 – 1926

23. *Latrobe and Slavery's Curse*

VIRGINIA in the early nation was a strange anachronism: the prime advocate of independence among the 13 states, yet the scene of black slavery. European travelers to the newly federated states were shocked by the inconsistency of Jefferson's Declaration of Independence and the slave markets they found in Richmond, Norfolk, and other Southern cities.

Young Benjamin Latrobe was no exception. This talented European architect sailed into Hampton Roads in 1795 from England, hoping to live in Virginia and design buildings. However, after three unprofitable years he moved on to Philadelphia and to Washington. It was Virginia's loss, for Latrobe was America's first fully professional architect.

Latrobe's early experiences in Tidewater, published as *The Virginia Journals of Benjamin Henry Latrobe, 1795–1798*, depict the best and worst of Virginia at the height of her power. Virginians like Washington, Jefferson, Madison, Monroe, and Marshall were truly national figures.

True, Latrobe seems to say, but beneath all that there was slavery. "Virginia ladies are delicate in the highest degree," Latrobe wrote from Richmond in 1797 after a talk with Governor James Wood's wife. "I prefer their manners without exception to those of the women of any country I was ever in. Were I to choose a wife by manners I would choose a Virginian." However, he adds, "There are things done and seen in Virginia which would shock the delicacy of a bold Englishwoman, a free Frenchwoman, and a wanton Italian." He meant slavery.

"What do you think, Madam," he wrote Mrs. Wood, "of the naked little boys running about every plantation? What do you think of girls and women, waiting upon your daughters in presence of gentlemen, with their bosoms uncovered? What think you of the known promiscuous intercourse of your servants, the perpetual pregnancies of your young servant girls, shamefully exhibited to your children?"

Latrobe blamed Virginians for tolerating what he felt was an inhumane system that made slaves "outcasts of the moral, as well as of political world"—subhuman creatures whose "love is on a level with those of the dogs and cats."

Latrobe had first been attracted to America from England by his admiration for Jefferson. But once in Virginia, he was dismayed to see

Painting by Sydney King, courtesy of
Jamestown-Yorktown Foundation

Governor Berkeley's Green Spring stood near Jamestown from about 1670 until razed about 1800.

what slavery did to Virginians, white and black. Although he was kindly received in Norfolk, Richmond, and on Tidewater plantations he visited, he found Virginia life fatally flawed. Our independence, generosity, and friendliness to strangers couldn't offset slavery.

Latrobe's Virginia journals, published in 1979 by Yale University Press, bring together everything the architect wrote and sketched in his three Virginia years. There you find his familiar painting of Green Spring plantation, near Jamestown, which Latrobe examined for its owner, William Ludwell Lee, who wanted to

raze it and build a new house. (Latrobe thought Lee stingy and pulled out, leaving Lee to find another architect.) There is also Latrobe's watercolor picture of the ruined Nelson House at Yorktown, still cannon-riddled 15 years after Cornwallis's surrender. There are countless other quick pen sketches or watercolors, always vivid and revealing.

Latrobe found upland Virginia more prosperous. His journeys introduce judges, merchants, and planters he met as he roamed the counties. He went to horse races, foxhunts, court days. He sketched insects, tobacco boats, slave markets, and field hands raising tobacco.

The years from the Revolution to the Civil War, which Latrobe partly spanned, were crucial for Virginia. Slavery was stunting Virginia's economy, retarding its progress. Abolitionist and antislavery feeling forced Virginia and the other slave states into defensiveness. Slavery seemed unAmerican.

Maryland Historical Society

Benjamin Latrobe depicted slaves at Fredericksburg among his Virginia views.

Latrobe's career took off after 1803, when his idol, President Jefferson, made him Surveyor of Public Buildings in Washington. Besides rebuilding the U.S. Capitol, Latrobe designed the Bank of the United States in Philadelphia and the Catholic cathedral in Baltimore. When he died of yellow fever in New Orleans in 1820 while developing that city's waterworks, he was famous. With Jefferson, he had made classical architecture popular throughout our growing nation.

Of all the buildings Latrobe designed in Virginia, the Richmond penitentiary (now greatly altered) is the best-known survivor. His fame survives more substantially through his handiwork on the Capitol in Washington. Too bad that Virginia couldn't make use of his talent.

24. *Benjamin Ewell to the Rescue*

S OME heroes are born," the saying goes, "and others are made." Benjamin Ewell, the Civil War president of William and Mary, didn't want to be a hero, but the war and Reconstruction forced it on him. Several times he tried to pass the presidency to others and to return to teaching, but fate wouldn't let him.

Ewell ended up devoting 35 years to the job. He served longer than any of William and Mary's 24 presidents except James Blair, who held out for 50 years, and Bishop James Madison, who served 35 years. To me, the bearded West Pointer who kept William and Mary together through two fires and a devastating war is the most appealing of Williamsburg personalities.

Legend has it that Ewell was a stern old codger who drove to Williamsburg from his farm at Ewell every day of the six years the college was closed and kept its spirit alive by tolling its bell. He was "old Buck," a wizened Mister Chips, beloved by young and old.

That stereotype is true, as far as it goes. But, as always, the truth is more complex than legend. The true Ewell was a gentle, conciliatory, driven man with a passion for the tidiness of mathematics and engineering. Beyond these qualities, he had leadership and personal worth that forced him into the college presidency and—during the Civil War—into service as an officer of the Confederacy.

In private, Ewell was a fatherly, domestic figure who enjoyed good company. Alas, however, a rift between him and his younger Pennsylvania-born wife, Julia McIlvaine Ewell, led her to leave Williamsburg soon after their daughter Lizzie was born and to go home to her parents in York, Pennsylvania. Not until after Benjamin Ewell died at 84 in 1894 did Julia Ewell return to Williamsburg.

Although Ewell attended West Point along with Robert E. Lee, Pierre Beauregard, and other Civil War leaders, he had family ties with William and Mary. An ancestor of his was Richard Heath of Northumberland County, who in 1776 was one of the five founders of Phi Beta Kappa at the college.

Military talent ran in the Ewell family. His maternal grandfather, Benjamin Stoddert, had been secretary of the Navy under John Adams. Both Ben Ewell and his more famous brother, General Richard Ewell, trained at West Point. Ben graduated third in his class in 1832 and

Colonial Williamsburg

President Ewell taught students in the President's House after the college closed.

Richard in 1840. Regarded today as one of the Confederacy's best talents, Lieutenant General Richard Ewell served under Jackson and succeeded to his command after Jackson died. He led Lee's advance at Gettysburg and defended Richmond in 1865 at the war's end.

A strong influence on the two men was their mother, Elizabeth Stoddert Ewell. She had been widowed and spent much time in Williamsburg during her son's presidency. In the absence of Ewell's wife, his mother was his housekeeper until she died in 1859.

Preferring teaching to military life, Ben Ewell stayed on at West Point after graduation to teach mathematics. A fellow cadet described him as "lenient and forgiving, almost to weakness," but he turned this to good effect. After West Point

he taught at Hampden-Sydney and at Washington College (now Washington and Lee), where he held the prestigious Cincinnati Society professorship of math and military science.

When William and Mary in 1848 suspended classes for a year because of a faculty dispute, its Board of Visitors invited 38-year-old Professor Ewell of Lexington to become president and to rebuild the school before reopening it. The Visitors offered him a "$1,000 salary, an excellent house in the college yard . . . and a spacious garden." He came, saw, and conquered.

When Ewell had the college ready to reopen, the Visitors engaged Bishop John Johns as president to serve without salary. Ewell stayed on to teach math but was prevailed on by the Visitors to accept the presidency again in 1854, when Johns had to resign because of his church duties. That year saw the resumption of Ewell's presidency, spanning three and one-half decades.

Ewell's first crisis was the accidental burning of the college building in 1859. So high was college morale, however, that he and his Board of Visitors raised $35,000 to add to the $20,000 insurance and reconstructed the building. It was barely completed before the Civil War erupted and the college closed. Ewell became a lieutenant colonel in the Virginia infantry, serving under General John Bankhead Magruder to erect Peninsula defenses against invasion. When General Joseph E. Johnston took over from Magruder in 1862, Ewell became one of Johnston's officers.

No college suffered greater loss than William and Mary in the Civil War. Drunken Federal troops burned the college building in 1862—the second burning in four years. Although Ewell reopened the school six months after Appomattox, it ran downhill until it closed again in 1881.

That was Buck Ewell's greatest challenge,

and he rose to it magnificently. Though 71 and dependent on his James City County farm, he was determined the college would not die. With the help of a Massachusetts congressman and a few ex-West Pointers (Ulysses Grant and Ambrose Burnside among them), he obtained donations to keep the nation's second oldest college alive. His success was later to inspire J. A. C. Chandler and the Rev. W. A. R. Goodwin.

Ewell sought annually after 1865 to have Congress reimburse William and Mary for the Federals' burning of the college in 1862. Each Congress in the 1870s and 80s seemed ready to act, but each time anti-Southern bitterness rose up and killed the appropriation, until 1893. Congress's $64,000 indemnification of the college in that year—the 200th anniversary of William and Mary's founding—was a glorious capstone to Ewell's career.

The old man died at Ewell Hall the next year and was buried next to his mother in the college cemetery. His life was summed up by his successor, President Lyon Tyler, in the college quarterly:

In Ewell's lifetime, Duke of Gloucester Street was unpaved. At the far end is the college.

Colonial Williamsburg

DIED, Tuesday, June 19, 1894, BENJAMIN S. EWELL, LL.D., Fellow of the Royal Society, President Emeritus of William and Mary College, and late Colonel of the Thirty-second Regiment, Virginia Volunteers, C.S.A. He was truly a remarkable man. Though eighty-four years of age, he retained almost to the last his brilliant powers of conversation and inexhaustible fund of cheerfulness and wit. The college was put in mourning for his loss, and his body was deposited in the college burying ground. . . .

In the long roll of William and Mary's sons and daughters, I am drawn magnetically to this modest man. "Old Buck" just wanted to teach math, but destiny forced him to be a hero.

Valentine Museum

A Confederate picket on lookout at Diascund Creek near Williamsburg painted his own portrait in 1862. He was Conrad Wise Chapman of Alexandria.

25. *The Yankees Arrive*

INFORMERS and spies of both North and South haunted Williamsburg from the time it was captured by General George B. McClellan's Union army on May 5, 1862, until Ulysses Grant finally invaded the Confederate capital of Richmond three bloody years later.

A rare view of those days was provided by Major David E. Cronin in his unpublished memoirs, which he wrote in old age, 40 years after Appomattox. A typescript of the narrative was later bought from Cronin's sister by the late Dr. W. A. R. Goodwin, who conceived the Williamsburg restoration. It is a mine of information about the historic town which stood midway between the Union bastion at Fort Monroe, to the east, and the Confederacy's heart at Richmond, to the west. More importantly, Cronin's narrative is a revealing insight into the hearts of the town's imprisoned citizens and their northern occupiers. It is dramatic, sad, and moving in turn—a rich, but little-known account of three terrible years.

After Virginia seceded from the Union in April 1861, the Virginia Peninsula became a main battleground of the oncoming war. Lincoln's army moved swiftly to strengthen Fort Monroe and to land advance troops to fortify Hampton and Newport News. Soon McClellan, Lincoln's top field general, came down from Washington to take over the buildup of 125,000 federal troops, determined to capture Richmond and to end the rebellion in a hurry.

Military headquarters in the Williamsburg of the Civil War were in the Palmer House, as it is now known, a beautiful colonial residence at the east end of Duke of Gloucester Street, across from the colonial Capitol. In those years the mansion was owned by W. W. Vest, the town's richest merchant, who had doubled the original brick structure into the largest and finest in town. After the Yankees had captured nearby Yorktown, Vest and his family fled with many other Williamsburgers to Richmond for safety.

That was when Confederate General John Bankhead Magruder, who had originally commanded the Peninsula's defenders, moved into the Vest house. He was soon succeeded there by General Joseph E. Johnston, who took over the Peninsula's defenses for the Confederacy.

On May 4, 1862, McClellan brought much of his Peninsula army to bear on Fort Magruder, the centerpiece of the Confederate defense line just east of town. After severe fighting all day, Johnston on the night of May 5 signalled his smaller force to retreat, abandoning Williamsburg.

Thus McClellan moved into the Vest house on May 6 for a few peaceful days before he started west in pursuit of Johnston. After that, Williamsburg and the Vest house remained for the rest of the war in the hands of Union occupiers. The town was a tenuous link between Federal armies fighting in Virginia and Fort Monroe, that "Union dagger at the heart of the Confederacy."

David Edward Cronin came to the former Virginia capital as a captain of the First New York Mounted Rifles. Well educated, he had been trained in Europe as an artist, and a collection of the pen-and-ink illustrations he drew in Williamsburg are in the New-York Historical Society. They don't compare with those which combat artist Winslow Homer was drawing at the same time for *Harper's Weekly*, but they're good.

"Probably no other building occupied as field headquarters in the war was continuously retained for so long," he wrote of the Vest house. "Strange to say, the furniture, fixtures, and belongings were kept in good condition, virtually intact."

The young officer appreciated the many beautiful old buildings of Williamsburg. According to Cronin, Williamsburg had been considered by the Continental Congress in 1779 as a possible capital of the 13 states. "Virginia tendered the site of Williamsburg," he wrote, "offering to turn over the Capitol and 300 acres of land, together with a cash bonus of $500,000 to be used in building 13 hotels for the use of the delegates in Congress."

Cronin gives a folksy view of McClellan, sitting in the conservatory of the Vest house writing to his wife. "This is a beautiful little town," McClellan wrote her. "Several very old houses and churches. Pretty gardens. I have possession of a very fine house which Joe Johnston occupied. It has a lovely flower garden and conservatory. If you were here, I would be much inclined to spend some time here."

Author's collection

The Vests' house on Duke of Gloucester Street was briefly General McClellan's headquarters.

But war is hell, and McClellan had to move on. However, pickets continued to surround the town to seal it off from possible Confederate spies and informers. Until Appomattox, Williamsburg was virtually a prison. Whites had to take oaths of loyalty. Food was scarce, and mail was censored. Rarely could a townsman get a permit to go to Yorktown, Norfolk, or other nearby towns held by the Federals.

On the weekly market day, Williamsburgers, both black an white, swarmed to an open-air market on Richmond Road to buy produce brought in by farmers from James River and York River farms. A few Williamsburgers now and then managed to slip letters and copies of the *Richmond Enquirer* past the pickets. Cronin and his troops kept busy trying to prevent that and the passing of signals and even an occasional Confederate spy between the Peninsula and Richmond. Messages were conveyed by gestures and semaphore. Once Cronin's police found a Confederate mail pouch secreted among the tombs beneath the chapel of the College of William and Mary, awaiting a pickup.

"For nearly two years Williamsburg was the nearest post to Richmond held by Union troops," Cronin wrote. "It became in this period a point of observation in the military line drawn about the Confederacy—a principal channel in securing the latest Confederate news, sometimes of great value at Washington."

Some Confederate messages were carried by blacks, who were exempt from oaths and restrictions imposed on white Confederate sympathizers. Other blacks secretly served the Union cause. Cronin exulted in the skill of Milly, a black maid of Richmond's leading unionist spy, Elizabeth Van Lew. Miss Van Lew often lent Milly to Mrs. Jefferson Davis, whose household unknowingly provided important intelligence to be sent by Miss Van Lew to Washington—sometimes by way of Williamsburg.

Williamsburg's Confederate internees risked a worse fate by sending frequent signals of Union movements to Confederate signalmen stationed in tall pine trees beyond the picket lines, outside of town. The tree-top signalmen then passed them to other signalmen far away. "By means of secret signals," Cronin learned, "messages were exchanged both day and night between the Confederates and their friends in town, who gave prompt warning of any increase of force or apparent movement on the part of the Unionists."

Cronin discovered after the war was over that three lovable black servants who looked after him in the Vest house were all carrying military secrets to their Confederate owners.

When the ex-soldier came back to Williamsburg in 1901, then a man in his 60s, he sought out and talked with a few aged survivors of those years. They could speak their hearts at last. But by then the three servants were dead. "All had obtained passes beyond the lines of

By Major David Cronin,
from New-York Historical Society

A Federal artist painted a Civil War skirmish at William and Mary in April 1863.

this world," he wrote, expressing hope that they "may find an all-forgiving governor at Elysian headquarters."

The biggest threat to Cronin's peacekeepers were marauding Confederate scouts, who roamed the Peninsula in search of chance Union targets. It was a Confederate scout's raid on the Federal garrison in the Wren Building at the college that provoked a drunken Pennsylvania soldier to set fire to the building in retaliation.

No love was lost between Williamsburg's jailers and its inmates. "The expression on the faces of Williamsburg people was one of undisguised hatred and contempt," Cronin wrote after 1901. "If ever there had been the least spark of Union sentiment in the place, that spark was wholly extinguished before the war was long in progress."

The town's only avowed native Unionist, lawyer Lemuel Bowden, served the Federal invaders in 1862 as a hated "puppet" mayor. Later that year Bowden was chosen by the Wheeling Convention as a United States senator, but he died of smallpox shortly thereafter in Washington.

Young David Cronin was a loyal Unionist, but he sympathized with the plight of the many women, children, and elderly men cooped up in Williamsburg. The provost marshal kept busy trying to avert pillage and vandalism by irresponsible soldiers in the Federal garrison force.

Cronin was indignant at the desecration of the papers of Governor John Page, a Revolutionary leader, after Page's son-in-law and daughter, Dr. and Mrs. Robert Saunders, had abandoned their house next door to the Governor's Palace. After inventorying numerous letters found in the Saunders house to Page from Washington, Jefferson, Lafayette, and others, Cronin had them boxed and sent to Fort Monroe to be given to libraries. However, most of the letters ended up in private hands. A few have been bought in recent years by Williamsburg libraries from dealers and auctions.

The provost marshal also reported the pilfering of engraved silver identification plates from the tombs of early colonial officials, removed from the William and Mary chapel crypt. He was pleased to learn of their return after the war.

In the final pages of his memoirs, Cronin describes his return to Williamsburg in 1901. The town was no larger than the 1,500 population of 1865, but it had a railway, the Chesapeake and Ohio, and a new inn. "An air of venerable prestige pervades the town, and this will always render it attractive and inspiring to lovers of history," he wrote.

So indeed it does.

26. *General McClellan Fails*

THEY called him "Young Napoleon" in 1861 when President Lincoln named him to lead the Army of the Potomac in the Civil War, but a year later General George B. McClellan was written off as a failure when his giant 125,000-man force failed to capture Richmond and the Confederate capital there. That's why McClellan is a minor historical figure compared to Generals Robert E. Lee and Ulysses S. Grant.

Scholars are still rehashing the Peninsula Campaign, which began with high hopes when McClellan landed at Yorktown in April 1862. After a muddy march up the Peninsula in May and June, "Little Mac's" army attacked Richmond in June and July. Many trenches dug before and during the four months of battles are visible on the Peninsula today. But nothing can convey the sheer horror of those bloodbath battles east of Richmond, now the area of Richmond's airport.

In the end, McClellan proved too cautious to defeat Virginia's aroused defenders. But Lee's army won those bloody Seven Days' Battles, and Lincoln later removed McClellan from top command. He resigned from the Army in 1864 to run against Lincoln for president, but he lost

that, too. He died in 1885, his fame obscured.

Criticism of McClellan began after he took command in Washington, even before he landed on the Peninsula. One critic was British war correspondent Frederick Edge, who sent weekly dispatches to London papers. In 1865, Edge's coverage was printed as a book and widely sold. Edge concluded that Democrats had seized on McClellan from the time of his promotion as a potential opponent to the Republican Lincoln in the 1864 presidential election. Edge charged that Democratic editors unfairly wrote that McClellan failed on the Peninsula because "Lincoln wouldn't send him enough troops."

The British journalist also charged that McClellan was absent from the field east of Williamsburg on May 5, 1862, when his army fought its first Peninsula action. "Had General McClellan been present," he asked, "is it not probable that the repulse of the Confederate army would have been turned into a total rout?" He also faulted "Little Mac" for settling into a comfortable Duke of Gloucester Street mansion after capturing Williamsburg on May 6 and remaining there a week. "Was there any reason whatever why McClellan should not have immediately followed the Confederate army across the Chickahominy?" he asked.

Throughout his narrative, Edge quotes Union soldiers' derision of McClellan for his indecision. "We might have bagged the whole crowd inside Yorktown if McClellan had had the pluck," Edge quotes one as saying. The Briton described the Peninsula as fiendishly hot, damp, and muddy in the spring rains of 1862. He found its roads impassable, and he deplored the Chickahominy's malarial swamps. But he liked plantation blacks, who gave the Yankees information on Confederate movements.

As McClellan's men approached Richmond, the British journalist wrote: "The rebel army at Richmond numbers some 125,000 men . . . many old, and all comparatively undrilled and undisciplined. . . . Large forts, built 10 years ago, surround [Richmond]," It was reported that many of Richmond's defenders lacked guns, carrying pikes instead. Actually, Lee's ill-equipped defenders of Richmond were fewer than 90,000 men and boys.

As McClellan delayed his attack on Richmond, Union soldiers asked each other, "Are we being humbugged, or is Joe Johnston really outgeneraling McClellan?" So reported Edge on May 26, from a point six miles from Richmond.

After McClellan lost the Battle of Seven Pines to the Confederates, Edge grew even more critical. McClellan's "invariable absence from the field of battle, his partiality for certain officers . . . upset the popularity manufactured so studiously for him by certain politicians and newspapers," he wrote.

The Briton reported that Confederates told him McClellan's army "might have marched into Richmond after the Battle of Seven Pines. They were utterly astonished at his unaccountable delay in following up his victory." General Joseph E. Johnston, the Confederate commander, was injured at Seven Pines, to be replaced by Robert E. Lee.

Edge criticized McClellan's permitting Mrs. Robert E. Lee and two of her daughters to come through federal lines from the Lee plantation,

Colonial Williamsburg

After a bloody battle, Federal forces entered Williamsburg and seized the city's government.

the White House, on the Pamunkey River. He noted that "officers of high rank complained" of McClellan's deference to "the wife of the principal rebel general" who presumably carried information on federal troops back to Lee. "Certain U.S. officers were wonderfully kid-gloved with these Southern aristocrats," he sneered.

Then came the bloody Seven Days' battles, from June 26 through July 2, with Lee taking the initiative. Casualties on both sides were high. Bodies lay unburied for days. In Richmond, tobacco warehouses were put to use as hospitals. Daunted by losses in battle, and by fevers, colds, and dysentery, McClellan stopped fighting on July 3 and encamped his army at Berkeley plantation on the James. There he was visited by the disappointed Lincoln, who had to try several other generals before Ulysses Grant in 1865 finally took Richmond.

McClellan complained all his life that the War Department had failed to reinforce his army, but critics pointed out that McClellan's forces greatly outnumbered his enemy. Edge concluded that "the young Napoleon" failed to make "good and sufficient use of the means already at his disposal." Indeed, the British cor-

Harper's Weekly illustration

Despite his "Young Napoleon" reputation, McClellan's Peninsula campaign failed.

respondent blamed McClellan's failure on his political ambition, together with "incompetency, want of energy and courage, or disbelief in his country's destiny."

27. *A Wartime Wedding*

ONE of Williamsburg's finest old houses is Bassett Hall, built in colonial times by the well-to-do Burwell Bassett. It is now a museum of the furnishings left there by John D. Rockefeller, Jr., and his first wife, Abby Aldrich. The house was also the scene of an unusual Civil War visit by Federal army Captain George Armstrong Custer to an injured Confederate officer Custer had known when the two were cadets at West Point.

One of McClellan's army captains in the Peninsular campaign of 1862 was Custer, who was to have a controversial career in the Army before he was killed with all his soldiers at the Battle of the Little Big Horn in Montana. By that time—14 years after his stay in Williamsburg—Custer was a national figure.

Williamsburg was filled with injured soldiers, both Yankee and Confederate, after the battle east of town. Some were hospitalized at the college, some at Bruton Church, and others in private homes. One of the battle's heroes was Dr. Robert Garrett, Williamsburg's physician, who tended many casualties at his home, the Coke-Garrett House.

Two injured Confederates were fortunate enough to be billeted in Bassett Hall, owned and occupied by Confederate Colonel Goodrich Durfey and his family. They were Captain John Willis Lea, 23, of the 5th North Carolina Regiment, and Lieutenant Hays. In her diary for May 20, 1862, Harriette Cary, a young Williamsburg friend of the Durfeys, described the two officers as "very interesting gentlemen . . . both doing quite well."

As a result of his visit, Captain Lea fell in love with the Durfeys' daughter, 18-year-old Margaret. After he recovered from his wounds, he was sent by the Federals to Fort Monroe, but they permitted him to come back to Bassett Hall to be married. He had obtained Margaret's father's permission, which was important in those days.

Captain Lea, the Confederate, then asked his West Point classmate, Captain Custer, the Yankee, to be best man. It was unusual, and apparently it took a little doing, for by August the Federal army had fought its way nearly to Richmond. There they had been repulsed and then had come back down the Peninsula to rest. Fortunately, it was possible for Custer to take leave in this lull and to join the Durfeys and his friend "Gimlet" Lea for the wedding and several days of post-nuptial sociability.

Colonial Williamsburg

Captain George Custer, USA, took part in the wedding at Bassett Hall.

In a letter to his sister, Custer described the wedding:

I was at the residence of the bride long before the appointed hour. Both [the bride and her cousin, Maggie, the bridesmaid] were dressed in white with a simple wreath of flowers upon their heads. I never saw two prettier girls. Lea was dressed in a bright new rebel uniform trimmed with gold lace; I wore my full uniform of blue. The minister arrived, and at nine we took our places upon the floor. Lea made the responses in a clear and distinct tone. The bride made no response whatever except to the first question; she was evidently confused, though she

afterwards said (laughingly) that she neglected to respond purposely so as to be free from any obligations.

Etched in a window pane of the morning room at Bassett Hall is the date of the wedding, "Friday, May 23, 1862." Sentimentalists believe Captain Lea did it with his wife's diamond ring.

In the Williamsburg summer, the young people amused themselves with card games and singing, among other things. Custer "never had so pleasant a visit among strangers," he wrote. The bride's cousin Maggie sang and played Southern songs like "Dixie" and "For Southern States, Hurrah" on the piano. Custer and Lea played card games while the bride and bridesmaid watched, Custer complaining that Lea "won every time. When playing for the Confederacy, he represented the South, I the North." After two weeks Custer rejoined Federal forces. Soon Lea too had to leave his bride and Williamsburg. He was exchanged for a Federal prisoner held by the Confederates, was wounded again at Chancellorsville and at Winchester, but was back again in the Confederate army at Appomattox when Lee surrendered to Grant.

After the war, Lea attended Virginia Episcopal Seminary at Alexandria, was ordained, and served parishes in Virginia and West Virginia until he died in 1884 at the age of 46. His wife had died a year earlier.

As for George Custer, bravery in battle and a flair for self dramatization won him a brigadier's command in June 1863—only 10 months after the wedding. It made him the youngest general in the Union army and led to his colorful postwar Indian fighting career. In the reorganization of the Army after the war, he was sent west to Indian territory to keep the peace and force tribal Indians onto governmental territories.

There Custer had a hectic career, once being court martialed for leaving his command without permission. He was reinstated, however, chiefly through his friend General Philip Sheridan.

Custer and his regiment were annihilated by

the Indians at the Little Big Horn in June 1876. Not realizing the number of the Indians, he divided his regiment in three parts to attack. In the massacre which followed, all were killed. They were buried on the battlefield, which is now a national monument. Custer himself was later re-interred at West Point, where he remains an anomalous figure in the history of the United States.

If you visit Bassett Hall you can still see the Leas' inscribed wedding date on a window pane. It is part of the legacy of one of Williamsburg's historic houses.

Colonial Williamsburg

Bassett Hall, one of Williamsburg's finest houses, was the scene of a Civil War wedding.

28. *The College Befriended*

IN July of 1882 the war-battered College of William and Mary—the nation's second oldest college and Williamsburg's chief remaining distinction—was forced to close. The college's board of visitors announced that the closing was temporary, designed to give the bankrupt school time to raise funds and repair its campus. Though it had been endowed originally by the British crown in 1693 and had been administered until the Revolution by the Church of England, the college since then had had to depend on its own slender resources. The Civil War had exhausted these.

The closing especially disappointed William and Mary's president, the 72-year-old Benjamin Stoddert Ewell. Ewell recommended to his board of visitors that they ask the General Assembly to make the college a normal school to train teachers for Virginia's post-Civil War public schools. Nothing came of Ewell's proposal until the 1887–88 session of the General Assembly. In that session, young delegate Lyon Gardiner Tyler of Richmond, a son of President John Tyler, successfully led an effort to subsidize the college with $10,000 annually, thus enabling the college to reopen in October 1888.

While William and Mary was closed, Ewell kept an office in the President's House in the college yard, where he looked after college affairs and properties. As he had been doing ever since the Civil War's end, he wrote letters for funds to revive the school. From Congress he sought money to repair its main building, now known as the Wren Building. In addition, Ewell sought help from northern capitalists, Civil War leaders (some of whom he had known at West Point), and even from Britons whom he presumed to be interested in the college begun by the British crown.

While the college slumbered, Ewell lived at his James City County farm, Ewell Hall, four miles north of the college on the Richmond stage road. There also lived his daughter Lizzie and her husband, Beverley Scott. Ewell's black servant, Malachi Gardiner, drove him to Williamsburg on weekdays in a carriage and helped him at the college and at home. Ewell's young wife, the former Julia McIlvaine, had deserted him before the war to return to her home in York, Pennsylvania, not to return in his lifetime. Lizzie therefore served as her father's housekeeper and hostess.

In May 1887 President Ewell received a visit from Daniel Coit Gilman, president of Johns

Hopkins University in Baltimore. Gilman was accompanied to Williamsburg by his wife, the former Elizabeth Dwight Woolsey of Connecticut, whom he called Lillie, and by Alice, his daughter by his first wife, the former Mary Ketcham. The three had embarked at Baltimore, docking the next day at Old Point Comfort. From there they had come by the Chesapeake and Ohio Railway's Peninsula line to Williamsburg. They took rooms in the town's best hostelry, the City Hotel, a clapboard structure at the northeast corner of the courthouse green on Duke of Gloucester Street, where they remained two days before returning to Baltimore.

Daniel and Elizabeth Gilman each wrote an account of the Williamsburg visit, both of which have survived. Gilman made two pages of abbreviated notes in his diary and on his return to Baltimore also wrote Ewell his thanks for the visit and Ewell's gift of books. Mrs. Gilman sent a fuller account to her sisters in Stratford, Connecticut. Gilman noted in his diary that "Lillie letters to her sisters, ret[urne]d to me, have a vivid description of all this."

A fuller description of the sleepy Williamsburg of 1887 was included in Elizabeth Gilman's letters. They were found later among the Gilmans' papers by President Gilman's daughter, Elizabeth. In March 1934 she had the portions relating to Williamsburg copied and sent them with an accompanying letter to John D. Rockefeller, Jr., whose plans to restore Williamsburg to its eighteenth-century form had been announced in 1928. Elizabeth Woolsey Gilman's account follows:

At Williamsburg we found a carriage and a very pleasant gentleman waiting to receive us. The carriage to be sure had a large hole in the floor thro' which A. warned me not to precipitate myself, but with a little precaution all went well and nothing could exceed the kind courtesy of our welcomer who proved to be also our host. Mr. Spencer, an F.F.V. and college graduate who keeps the hotel of the village and does it like a gentle-

Ferdinand Hamburger, Jr. Archives,
the Johns Hopkins University

Daniel Coit Gilman, president of Johns Hopkins University, visited Williamsburg in 1887. He is shown with his sister Louisa, left; his first wife; and his daughter Alice.

man. We found nice airy rooms with very clean muslin curtains and pillow covers, and a parlor with Chippendale chairs and old family portraits (one by Sully) and various other signs of better days. The table linen, glass and china were delicately fresh and our table adorned with lovely fresh flowers, and the fare remarkably good for a country inn.

We were received by a charming old colored woman who showed us our rooms and brought us fresh water, etcetera. She had a fine face full of force and her manner was just

Colonial Williamsburg

The college looked barren from Jamestown Road when Gilman visited in 1887.

that mixture of respect and familiarity which one hears of in the best of the old family servants before the war. That is exactly what she is. She was Mrs. Spencer's "Mammy", never left the family and is now helping to bring up Mrs. Spencer's children and to run the hotel for Mrs. Spencer's benefit. "I could have hugged the obsolete old woman!"

As soon as we, with "Mammy's" assistance, had disposed of some of the dust, we ascended once more with care into our carriage and drove all about the little town. It used to be the centre of an elegant wealthy country aristocracy living freely in a handsome way in their fine old houses and everywhere are signs of the former life and elegance all gone to decay. Imagine a southern Stratford [Connecticut] with oaks and maples instead of the elms—many of the houses

finer than any of the Stratford houses, but instead of that air of decorous well kept respectability everything ruined and out of repair. The streets a foot deep in dust and worn in holes and ruts. Many of the old houses shut up and going to decay—others with rotting gate posts and broken chimneys and hanging shutters, still occupied by the last lingering relics of the old families who once lived in gay state and splendor.

The old colonial church covered with beautiful ivy is still opened every other Sunday for service and inside has been tastelessly renovated. It contains the font in which Pocahontas is said to have been baptized, and various old tablets on the wall attest to the learning and politeness of many worthies of the early part of the last century. One of them was so very worthy and polite that we are told that the Governor of the Province and various other officials stood in "teares" when he was committed to the tomb. Outside the walls are disintegrating fast tho' the splendid old masonry will hold awhile longer.

The church stands in an English churchyard full of beautiful tombs all dropping to pieces. Some of them go back over two hundred years. It almost brought tears to my eyes to read of the "inconsolable sorrow" of the husbands and children and wives who had so long ago buried their loved ones here, and thought how long ago those tears had been wiped away. The trees and the grass grow thick there and the roses here and in every door yard of the place simply run riot. Every mouldering old chimney had its ivy and its ambitious rose bush clambering after it and every old fence was borne down with vines and shrubs and roses and syringas. The air was heavy with fragrance.

We drove to the college grounds. Here too all was silence and desolation. The grass grows high and the trees are all untrimmed and the buildings look sad and neglected enough. An old colored woman who seemed to be the sole guardian told us that Col. Ewell was out at "the farm" and as we still had a few hours of daylight left we thought we would drive out and let him know of our arrival as we had been in communication with him about our visit. It was four miles, and four miles of Virginia roads, which means that we often had to go at a walk and that we arrived yellow with dust from head to foot.

Peter Ash [Epps], our driver, however, was equal to the emergency. He had no idea of his people presenting themselves in any such plight, and before we drew up he hailed a small colored boy and told him to bring him a whisk so that as each in turn alighted Peter with earnest vigor nearly brushed his or her clothes off his or her back. We were received by the old Colonel very warmly and by his daughter, Mrs. Scott, a lovely woman with

sweet manners. She had just come in from feeding her turkeys and digging in the garden. The next day she and her father came in and showed us some of the antiquities of the place and opened the old buildings and showed us the dusty old books and pictures.

It is a most pathetic place, full of the past with no present but one of dreary decay, and no future. The poor old college has been burnt several times, and has grown poorer and poorer until it could not longer support a faculty, so the students have gone and Colonel Ewell, the last President, is left alone. Once a year he rings the bell to let the world know that Old William and Mary still is ready to do its part in the education of youth. The rest of his time he gives to hopeless efforts to rouse once more the dead and gone public interest. The public has long ago forgotten all about poor old William and Mary and the cows are grazing peacefully in the playgrounds and the old walls are crumbling away and when the old Colonel goes, I suppose all traces of the place will gradually disappear. It seems as if it ought to be kept as a historic monument, if nothing else, being associated with Washington, Jefferson, Monroe, Madison, Tyler, Marshall and others.

The old Colonel drives in every day over the four dusty miles to see visitors and answer letters. His attendant is always a little black boy named Malachi whom the Colonel calls "Professor!" Malachi carries all the keys and unlocks and locks up the doors and knows just where to find the books needed. His little heart is all occupied with the old place and if for any reason the Colonel is prevented from coming in, Malachi feels the responsibility of the possible visitors' disappointment deeply. He knows all the musty old college jokes and when the Colonel showed us in the old record book of a hundred years and more ago the wanton deeds of lads who have been gone a century, Malachi respectfully buried his face in his little woolen cap and when he

Colonial Williamsburg

Lafayette visited Williamsburg in 1824 as a guest of Mrs. Mary Monro Peachy.

found he positively could bear no more of "ye sprightly boyes" he tiptoed into the hall to titter. The rest of the time he sat like a little black statue except for the wriggling of his funny little bare toes. He brought A. and me each a bunch of quite overblown roses from the farm and when we came away he ran after us to ask "is you comin back dis way from Richmond?" and on our answering in the negative he said "Cos if you is I'd bring you a whole basket full of roses," so we were friends.

So we were with Peter Ash [Epps], our driver, a very fine looking negro who knew everything about the town from its earliest settlement to the present day. He knew every old house and every one in it. It was 'ole' Miss this, or 'ole doctor' that, or 'ole' Major, or 'ole' Colonel. They were all old, nobody was new. He knew just where every cannon ball had struck every chimney and showed us

and told us everything. When Peter is not driving the carriage he waits on the table in a white jacket and apron and converses with great freedom in such a sweet round voice that it was a pleasure to hear him.

Peter told Mrs. Spencer "Miss Sally aint you goin up to see those ladies, they're grit." By this Peter meant that we were the real thing—no reference to the dust which he removed with such effort. Peter it seems is never taken in by false appearances of wealth and style but has an unerring instinct. So Mrs. Spencer came and spent the evening with us and most delightful she was. She does not live at the hotel but takes her meals there and I fancy gives the place the benefit of her advice and dainty touch. She still lives in the Peachy mansion where her ancestors have lived for several generations, and where her grandmother entertained LaFayette during his last visit. Certainly nothing more delightful could be wished than the picture she made sitting before us in a crisp white organdie trimmed with lace, her lovely white neck and throat covered with tulle and her head surmounted by an enormous white straw bonnet covered with white feathers. She sat swaying a huge turkey feather fan looking, I am sure, just like all her own grandmothers and talked to us in a sweet low voice full of unusual inflections and showed us old books and documents and altogether was, as I say, delightful.

I am, however, stealing Mr. [William Dean] Howells thunder for he had been there only a short time before. Mrs. Spencer was very funny over Mrs. Howells airs and graces, and her own utter indifference to Mr. Howells literary reputation. "He isn't very celebrated is he? At best he's only been so five or six years, hasn't he?" It is quite discreditable in Williamsburg to have a reputation only five or six years old.

After the Gilmans had returned to Baltimore, Daniel Coit Gilman wrote Benjamin Ewell to thank him for his hospitality and for books that Ewell had given him. His letter began:

Dear Colonel Ewell

Our visit to William and Mary has been the daily theme of our conversation ever since our return. For years I have looked forward to such an opportunity as we enjoyed under your guidance to see the old town, the historic college, the portraits, the books, the manuscripts, and the other relics which indicate what happy purposes and high hopes were brought to Virginia by the early settlers. . . . You seem to me the embodiment of the *genius loci,* the watchful and faithful guardian of a grand idea. As long as you live we may be sure the spark of fire will not disappear from the sacred altar. . . .

Soon after the Gilman's visit, Ewell's efforts to revive the college began to be rewarded. With the $10,000 annual subsidy voted by the General Assembly, William and Mary was able to plan its reopening. At Ewell's insistence that he was no longer equal to the presidency, the Board of Visitors then chose Tyler as its seventeenth president, and the college reconvened in October 1888. In 1893, in the college's 200th anniversary year, Congress voted $64,000 restitution for the burning of the Wren Building. The college was clearly reviving.

Until he died in 1908, Daniel Coit Gilman continued his interest in William and Mary, and in 1905 the college awarded him an honorary degree. Perhaps because of the attention paid the college by Gilman and by Herbert B. Adams, a Johns Hopkins history professor who in 1887 had written a pamphlet in support of William and Mary, several graduates of Johns Hopkins played a part in the college's renaissance. Among them were two of William and Mary's first faculty doctors of philosophy in history: John Lesslie Hall, who became the college's first dean under Lyon G. Tyler, and Julian Alvin Carroll Chandler, who succeeded Tyler as president.

In 1906, the Commonwealth of Virginia at last assumed financial responsibility for the onetime royal college, gradually restoring its original liberal arts character. The years of neglect that had forced the college's six-year closing are now all but forgotten.

29. *The Ladies Are Heard From*

ONCE every month some 15 or 20 Williamsburg ladies gather at one or another's house to consider the needs of the poor, aged, and ill in Williamsburg. The meeting starts with one member reading from a religious source and another offering the prayer of the order. Then they vote gifts of money or aid to needy cases. Finally, they let down their hair to talk and drink tea.

They're the Kate Custis Circle of the King's Daughters. Ever since 1888 they've been doling out firewood, Christmas baskets, and money to people black and white. "We're a mixture of good works, tea, and gossip," admits one member. "We're the oldest charity in Williamsburg and the oldest women's organization outside the churches." One big change is today's informality. In earlier years King's Daughters wore hats and gloves to meetings. Few do nowadays.

Williamsburg was recovering from the Civil War when Kate Custis in 1888 called together 10 friends to start a chapter of the Daughters, which had originated in New York in 1867. Besides Mrs. Custis, who ran a girls' school, members included Mrs. Charles Coleman, Mrs. Peyton Randolph Nelson, Mrs. Randolph Harri-

son, Mrs. Virginia Morecock, and Mrs. Thomas Jefferson Stubbs. One granddaughter and several other kinsmen of founders are members of the King's Daughters today, which is still a group of about 20. Their biblical motto is "Bear ye one another's burden and so fulfill the law of Christ."

Williamsburg was pitifully poor in 1888. The first King's Daughters paid dues of three cents a month, raised to five cents, and in 1919 to ten cents. Today's dues are $5, and legacies from former members add to the circle's giving.

Minute books of the Daughters' early years show that the membership has changed over the years but the style is the same. Members still keep in personal touch with Williamsburg's needy, both black and white. "We cut out the red tape so we can help in a hurry," says Mrs. Cara Dillard, a niece of Susan Garrett Nelson, one of the founders. "We don't have to consult anybody when people with needs call us up or come to see us for help."

In old-fashioned lined notebooks bearing handwritten minutes of the society's early years are listed donations approved at each meeting. On November 6, 1898, "It was resolved to buy for a coloured man who had both feet cut off by the train an entire shoemaker's outfit to assist him in making a living." Explains one member, "We've always believed the Lord helps them who help themselves."

A silver tea at the President's House at William and Mary in January 1895, is happily noted: "Perfect success. Made $9.10." The hostess was Mrs. Lyon Tyler, wife of the college's president from 1888 to 1918, and long-time president of the Daughters. Other presidents have included Mrs. Charles Coleman of the Tucker house, Miss Estelle Smith of the Brush-Everard house, Mrs. Randolph Harrison of the Wythe house, Mrs. Peyton Randolph Nel-

son of Tazewell Hall, and Mrs. R. B. Watts of Amblers on the James.

Mrs. Coleman called the group "the Princesses" because they were "Daughters of the King." Her daughter-in-law, the late Mrs. George Preston Coleman, and her granddaughter, Dr. Janet Kimbrough, were also long-time members.

Minutes for December 14, 1898, list a crop of new members: "Misses Lu Webb, Pet Lee, Pinky Morecock, Jennie Braithwaite, Mary Mercer, Anne Stubbs, Ella Moncure, Virgie Armistead, and Henrietta Booth." Miss Stubbs, daughter of Professor Thomas Jefferson Stubbs,

Association for the Preservation of Virginia Antiquities

Williamsburg ladies were upset when Jamestown was offered for sale by a realtor in 1899.

Colonial Williamsburg

The King's Daughters met often at the Tucker-Coleman house to aid charities.

Colonial Williamsburg

Cynthia Tucker Coleman, APVA founder, was a charter member of King's Daughters.

later married Ballard Boswell and was the society's secretary. She gave the past minute books to the Swem Library at the college with the circle's approval.

Christmas baskets for poor families were once a major activity. On December 20, 1916 the Daughters "met at Mr. Griffin's grocery store and packed pine baskets amounting to $2.10 each. Besides the baskets, $1 was set aside "to buy delicacies for an old coloured woman dying with cancer, $1 to be spent on four hot dinners for the old blind man at the gaol, and $1 for old William Frazier." Mrs. Braithwaite distributed the baskets from her carriage, driven by her coachman, Coldweather. Recipients were kept confidential. "We believe charity should be quiet," one member says.

The King's Daughters in early years made donations to causes like the Covington Home for Boys and Crippled Children's Home in Richmond. In 1934, before government welfare programs, it raised more than $1,000 to help the poor in Williamsburg. However, as welfare agencies developed, the King's Daughters simplified their program. "There's still some duplication," a member says, "but we can move faster than others."

Many ailments of charity recipients in early years, like pellagra, have died out. Other needs continue, however, like wood to keep home fires burning in winter and Meals on Wheels, which the Daughters support. When Williamsburg Community Hospital was built in the 1950s, the Daughters gave a meditation room. And before the hospital auxiliary was started there, Daughters worked at the hospital to write letters for patients and do other chores.

Though other chapters are coeducational and call themselves King's Daughters and Sons, the Kate Custis ladies have had only two male members, the late Mayor Henry M. "Polly" Stryker and Lyon Gardiner Tyler. "I don't think men would enjoy themselves much drinking tea with us," explains a current member.

And the tea-drinking continues. The minutes of October 12, 1926, record that "The meeting was adjourned, and a session over the teacups was enjoyed before disbanding." At another meeting, "The Circle adjourned to the green lawn and pleasant shade of Miss [Estelle] Smith's back garden, where cake, fruit punch, and neighbourly gossip closed the evening."

In the age of Medicare and Medicaid, the gentle ladies of the King's Daughters might seem unnecessary, but not really. "They give human qualities that the world can never get enough of," says one Williamsburg welfare worker. "They give love and personal contact."

I have a hunch that most Williamsburgers would agree.

30. *Williamsburg Memories*

JOHN Ruskin wrote that ruined buildings are more romantic than preserved ones. When I see photographs of pre-restoration Williamsburg, I'm touched by the gentle charm of the seedy little town that Mr. Rockefeller brought back to life after 1926.

I also enjoy accounts by long-dead Williamsburg people of what the town was like in earlier days. Typical are the memoirs of Mrs. Victoria King Lee, whose family fled their home in Hampton in 1861, before the Yankees came, and took refuge during the Civil War in Williamsburg. She lived the rest of her life in Williamsburg.

"Coming to a strange town," Victoria wrote, "it was natural that I, a young girl who had seldom been away from home, should take keen interest in my surroundings." As an old lady in the early 1900s, she wrote her memoirs for her family. They give an interesting insight.

In 1861 the roadway down the center of Gloucester Street—then always called Main Street—was like a country road. Footpaths took the place of present sidewalks, and grass grew from the edge of these paths almost to the center of the street. Cows grazed along the street as they pleased, and sometimes the passage of a carriage was delayed while a drove of pigs ran from a mud puddle in the road.

Almost every house had its pigpen, though most of the better class of people placed them further away from the houses than the corner of their front fences. The pigpens are gone now, but a number of smokehouses still stand, testifying to the fact that a pigpen once stood not far away.

Victoria Lee described a "dressing tree" on Richmond Road near the college: "At that time the poor country people who had to walk to town carried their shoes in their hands as they walked along the muddy country roads." They halted under the "dressing tree" to dust off their feet and put on their shoes and stockings before entering town.

Another memoir of Williamsburg was dictated by John S. Charles to his granddaughter before he died in 1930 at his home on Prince George Street. He was a kinsman of Newport News residents Roy Charles, Allen Charles, and Mrs. Thomas Newman. His recollections of buildings which stood in his lifetime greatly helped the Restoration in reconstructing some of them.

Born in 1851, John Charles moved to Williamsburg as a boy and attended private schools there. He was taught as a boy by Colonel Benjamin Ewell, president of the College of William and Mary, and he himself was principal of Matthew Whaley public school for 20 years before he died.

When John Charles knew Williamsburg in the Civil War and later, it had no sidewalks, no street lights, no bank, and no public schools. The C&O railroad livened things up after it came through in 1881. William and Mary had only its three original buildings. When the college closed from 1881 to 1888 for lack of money, President Ewell let Charles live in Brafferton Hall, one of the three buildings, as a sort of caretaker.

A third memoirist of the town was George Preston Coleman, mayor of Williamsburg from 1929 to 1934. Like John Charles, Coleman as a

Virginia Historical Society

A general store occupied a Duke of Gloucester Street corner, later to be Casey's site.

boy was taught by Colonel Ewell. After winning a law degree at William and Mary, he became Virginia's first highway boss but returned to Williamsburg in 1927 to become president of the Peninsula Bank (now part of the Crestar bank chain), which had been founded in 1898. Coleman lived through the start of the Restoration in the '20s and '30s.

I especially like Coleman's evocative description of Williamsburg in 1932:

> Williamsburg on a summer day! The straggling street, ankle deep in dust, grateful only to the chickens, ruffling their feathers in perfect safety from any traffic danger. The cows taking refuge from the heat of the sun, under the elms along the sidewalk. Our city fathers, assembled in friendly leisure, following the shade of the old courthouse around the clock, sipping cool drinks and discussing the glories of our past. Almost always our past!

> There were men and women who strained every nerve, every means in their power, to help the Williamsburg of the present day, to supply the necessities of life to poorer neighbors, to build up the college and procure means of education to their children, but even they shrank from looking toward the future. The past alone held for them the brightness which tempted their thoughts to linger happily. . . .

Well, all that has gone. Williamsburg today is a very different place. It's certainly more prosperous, but it's lost a lot of romance. John Ruskin was right. There's something about ruins. . . .

The Baptist Church near the Powder Magazine was a hospital after the Battle of Williamsburg.

Colonial Williamsburg

31. *Woodrow Wilson Pays a Call*

ONCE upon a time the Virginia Peninsula was a law-abiding place, where crimes were few and the president of the United States could walk the streets without a Secret Service man to guard him.

That's the way we were in July 1916 when President Woodrow Wilson came to Yorktown and Jamestown on the presidential yacht, *Mayflower*. He had become president in 1913, lost his first wife and married a second, and was trying to keep America out of World War I. Pressure on him was fearful, so his doctor persuaded him to escape the White House and cruise for a long weekend in Virginia.

With him came Lieutenant Commander Cary Grayson, a Navy medical officer whose duty was to look after Wilson's health. Grayson had graduated from William and Mary in 1899 and had then got his M.D. and joined the Navy Medical Corps. He'd become physician to the White House under Teddy Roosevelt and stayed on through the terms of William Howard Taft and Wilson.

Cary Grayson wrote about Wilson's visit to Yorktown in *Woodrow Wilson, an Intimate Memoir*, which first appeared in 1959 in the *Atlantic Monthly*, well after both men were dead. It is a refreshing bit of hero worship.

"One afternoon [the president] and I eluded the Secret Service men by saying that we were going to take a little trip in the motor launch," Grayson wrote of the 1916 visit to the Peninsula. "When we landed at Yorktown we left the sailors in the boat and struck out alone through the streets of the old town, which had practically gone to sleep at 3 o'clock in the afternoon, and made our way to the Court House." We can well believe it of Yorktown on a July afternoon.

"In one of the rooms an old man was sitting at a table writing in a deed book with his coat off, his suspenders much in evidence, and sucking on a corncob pipe," Grayson recalled. "The president asked if he could see the courtroom, and the old gentleman kept writing, and said, 'Yep, help youself. Go right upstairs.' The president said: 'May I ask who is your judge?' The reply was: 'D. Gardiner Tyler, son of the tenth president of the United States, brother of Lyon G. Tyler, president of William and Mary College. . . .'"

In the courtroom the president met T. T. Hudgins, clerk of the York County circuit court. Wilson didn't introduce himself, but a presiden-

William and Mary

World War I students at William and Mary stage a fire drill at the President's House.

1917 and father of the late Mrs. Leslie O'Hara, who lived until 1987.

Then, Grayson remembered, "We walked around Yorktown, went to the post office, bought some postcard pictures of the Custom House and of the Moore House, Washington's headquarters, and of the Nelson house. The postmaster who was also the storekeeper, wanted to know if we did not want to buy some 'pop' or ginger ale." Wilson said no.

Ambling along Yorktown's Main Street, Wilson noticed men sitting in chairs beneath a tree, "some half asleep, some exchanging random remarks, though no one recognized that the president was passing." Finally, a girl about 12 stopped and said, "Excuse me, sir, but you certainly do remind me of the pictures of President Wilson." When Wilson smiled young Catherine Sheild pounced. "You are President Wilson, are you not?" Answered Wilson, "Yes, I am guilty."

Catherine, later the wife of Vice Admiral John J. Ballentine, insisted on introducing Wilson to her mother, Mrs. Conway Sheild, Sr., who gave the visitors iced tea on her porch, later the residence of Judge Conway Sheild, Jr.

Catherine Sheild showed Wilson the Nelson House next door to her house and urged him to visit Yorktown Monument and the Moore House. To reach the latter, Wilson and Grayson went in their motor launch downriver to the Moore House waterfront, took off their shoes, rolled up their trousers and waded in. A bull was in the pasture, so Grayson made the president climb a fence.

Cary Grayson's narrative stops at that point, but we know the president's yacht later went from Yorktown around the lower Peninsula to Jamestown. There they got a ride with Charles Person of Williamsburg, who owned the town's only Buick, and drove into Williamsburg on a July Sunday afternoon. They stopped at the college because Wilson's wife, the former Edith Bolling, had known Anne Tucker, the wife of college president Lyon Tyler, when they had been girls in Wytheville. The Tylers greeted

tial poster bearing Wilson's picture hung right beside Hudgins. After President Wilson had examined some early record books, he and Grayson left. They learned later that Hudgins had indeed recognized Wilson but had respected his privacy. "There was a true gentleman," Wilson said. The clerk was Theophilus T. Hudgins, clerk of the circuit court from 1893 to them warmly and showed them the college and Bruton Church to which Wilson gave a Bible.

Cary Grayson then suggested that the Wilsons join him in a call in the afternoon on the Misses Lottie and Mary Garrett in the Coke-Garrett House. Miss Mary had been Grayson's Sunday school teacher at Bruton, and their brother, Dr. Van Garrett, had taught Grayson premedical courses at the college. Alas, the two ladies had gone out, so Grayson and the Wilsons left their cards.

Woodrow Wilson returned to Williamsburg nine months later to speak at William and Mary on the war. Despite his efforts to keep the United States neutral, Germany's unrestricted U-boat warfare was forcing the nation into the war. The United States finally declared war on April 6, 1917, a few days after Wilson's return to Washington.

Admiral Grayson, a Democrat, was chairman of Franklin Roosevelt's inaugural committee in 1933 and was appointed by Roosevelt in his last years to be president of the American Red Cross. He accompanied Roosevelt to Williamsburg in 1934 to speak at the inauguration of John Stewart Bryan as president of the college and to dedicate the restored Duke of Gloucester Street.

Grayson had been born on Salubria Farm at Brandy Station near Culpeper, the son of a country doctor. After he was orphaned at 12, he worked his way through William and Mary as assistant librarian and college postmaster. His skill as a horseman led President Teddy Roosevelt to select him from the Navy Medical Corps to ride with him in 1905 on a four-day "fitness" cavalcade from Washington into Virginia, covering about 40 miles a day. When Teddy's eyeglasses sleeted up, Grayson had to lead the blinded president. Senior military and naval officers who couldn't ride the course were required by the president to retire.

Outdoorsman Teddy was so impressed with the horseman that he invited Grayson to move to the White House as his physician. Besides, Grayson was an attractive, social fellow who

William and Mary

Lyon Tyler greeted President Wilson on his 1916 visit to the college.

entertained well at his Washington townhouse and at his Blue Ridge Farm at Upperville, where he bred and raced horses.

Grayson was a lively raconteur and friend of the great. On his death in 1938 at the age of 59, the *New York Times* wrote that "He was closer to Woodrow Wilson than any other man."

About the closest Cary Grayson ever came to indiscretion was when he characterized the medical disabilities of the three presidents he served. He said Teddy Roosevelt overexercised, Taft overate, and Wilson overworked. Each died of his excess.

William and Mary

Franklin Roosevelt spoke at the college in 1934 on the inauguration of John Stewart Bryan.

32. *Soldiers at Mulberry Island*

IN the first 300 years of Virginia's settlement, Williamsburg was a center of a farm economy that stretched between the James and York rivers in rural James City and York counties. Many of the earliest plantations fronted on the rivers and had wharfs for loading ships with tobacco, timber, and grain exports.

But farming declined in the twentieth century, and many farms were taken over for other purposes. Four major farming areas near Williamsburg were bought up by the Federal government in this century's World Wars. In World War I, Mulberry Island on the James became part of Fort Eustis, and a large tract on the York became the Yorktown Naval Weapons Station. In World War II the Navy added Cheatham Annex and the armed forces created Camp Peary, both in York County near Williamsburg.

Especially important historically was Mulberry Island, which was a James River port and village from Jamestown's day until Uncle Sam bought the island and nearby land in 1918 for the Army's Balloon Observation School and Coast Artillery Center. The island had been named by John Smith for its mulberry trees, and the 1918 fort was named for Brigadier

General Abraham Eustis, a Virginian who had set up the Army artillery school in 1824 at nearby Fort Monroe.

Fort Eustis has expanded greatly since 1918. Mulberry Island, which was at first important to the fort, is now merely a gunnery range. Might not the Army have spared the island and confined Fort Eustis to the adjoining mainland? But, alas, it's too late. The colonial church and seventeenth-century houses once on Mulberry are long gone. Their memory is kept alive only by a few local historians who are aware of the number of Virginia families going back to Mulberry Island.

The most important Mulberry Islanders were William Peirce, a first settler whose daughter, Jane, became John Rolfe's second wife after Pocahontas died in England, and Miles Cary, who came to Mulberry Island from England in 1645 and generated one of Virginia's prominent families. Most of the government and college buildings in eighteenth-century Williamsburg were built by two of Cary's descendants, Henry Cary, Sr. and Henry Cary, Jr.

Mulberry Island isn't big, but it once had an Anglican church (James Blair came monthly from Jamestown to preach) and several dozen

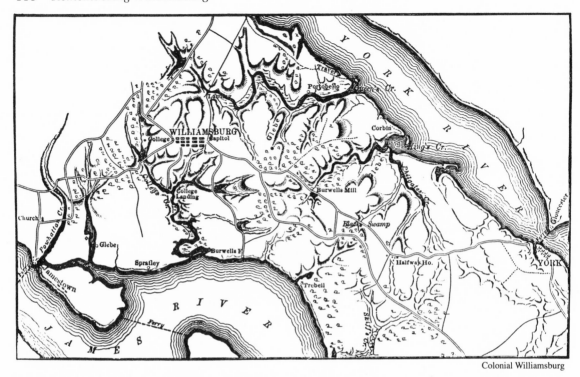

Colonial Williamsburg

Williamsburg was a trade center for eighteenth- and nineteenth-century rural plantations.

farmhouses. Residents of the Denbigh area of Newport News get a good view of the little island from across narrow Warwick River, which with Skiffe's Creek separates it from the mainland.

Dorothy Vollertsen of Williamsburg wrote interestingly about early Mulberry Island and about William Peirce and Miles Cary in a booklet she assembled with her late husband, Colonel Arthur Vollertsen, in 1983. Titled "The Carys and Peirces: Mulberry Island Families," it was published by the Fort Eustis Historical and Archaeological Association. It contains much data on interesting early Peninsula residents and on the life of Mulberry Island.

Skiffe's Creek and Warwick River gave Mulberry Island the protected harbor that early settlers needed, just as Jamestown, Archer's Hope, Hampton, and Yorktown did.

William Peirce lived there and as a sea captain sailed to England several times. After John Rolfe died in 1622—perhaps on Mulberry Island in the Indian massacre—Peirce, his father-in-law, was his executor. Peirce became captain of the Jamestown Fort in 1623 and then lieutenant governor of the colony. He also became a burgess, a member of the general court and then a member of the Virginia Council until he died in 1647, probably at Mulberry Island, where he acquired over 2,000 acres.

Miles Cary, the Mulberry Island settler best known to history, came to Virginia from England at age 22 in 1645. He married well and soon owned many thousands of acres in Warwick County, close to Mulberry Island.

Cary became the militia colonel of Warwick County and died fighting off an attack by Dutch ships at Old Point in 1667. His eroded gravestone bearing his coat-of-arms is the oldest in onetime Warwick County. He left four Warwick plantations, including Windmill Point, the Forest, and Magpie Swamp. His descendants, including councilors and governors, spread in colonial times to Hampton, Williamsburg, Richmond, and elsewhere, marrying with colonial planter families. However, there aren't many Carys left in Virginia today bearing that surname.

The Confederates in 1861 built Fort Crafford on Mulberry Island to deter Union ships on the James, but it was abandoned in 1862 when the Union army under General George B. McClellan invaded the Peninsula. Union forces pillaged the island's farms, which never regained their pre-war prosperity. Few people were left on Mulberry Island in 1918 when the Army created Fort Eustis.

One colonial house from the age of William Peirce and Miles Cary survives in Fort Eustis, close to the Warwick River. It is the Matthew Jones house, begun in the 1600s and enlarged about 1770.

In World War II Fort Eustis grew big as the home of the Army Transportation Command. As the base spreads, archaeologists try to see that important colonial sites known to be underground are investigated and preserved. Unfortunately, the burning of Warwick County records in the Civil War has destroyed nearly all of the area's records.

An early map of Mulberry Island and the adjoining Warwick River shore shows many picturesque local names that have disappeared: Joyle's Neck, Jail Creek, Saxon's Gaol, and my favorite, Butler's Gut. A "gut," in case you didn't know, can be a narrow channel. It's still there at Mulberry Island.

Clearly, wars and rumors of wars have greatly changed Williamsburg's surrounding countryside since 1607.

River steamers called at Mulberry Island on the James, now the site of Fort Eustis.

Mariners Museum

33. *Weyanoke on the James*

PLANTATIONS remind us that the early settlers of Virginia wanted to create dynasties, like those which had ruled the England they left behind. Weyanoke plantation in Charles City 30 miles up the Peninsula above Jamestown, is an example. After 370 years as a producing plantation, Weyanoke is today owned by a descendant of one of its early families.

He is Lawrence Lewis, Jr., a descendant of the Warner Lewises of Gloucester and the Fielding Lewises of Kenmore. They were relatives of George Washington.

To rediscover Weyanoke's lost years, today's Lawrence Lewis, Jr. engaged historian Ransom True to research and write about it. The result is *Plantation on the James*, a chronicle running from 1607 until 1938, when the father of the present owner bought back the family seat.

The most surprising fact about Weyanoke is that it has been cultivated off and on since 1717, when Chief Opechancanough, Powhatan's brother and successor, granted several thousand acres of land the Indians called "Weyanoke" to colonial Governor Sir George Yeardley. Yeardley proceeded to settle 26 English emigrants there in 1619—one of the westernmost English sites in Virginia of that day.

After the Virginia Indian massacre of 1622, the Weyanoke tribe of Indians reclaimed their land. About 1655 the grant was taken up again by Joseph Harwood, a new arrival from England. A shipyard and an early Charles City County courthouse were built there and Harwood also operated a tavern and a James River ferry. Subsequent generations of Harwoods built up the estate, selling their produce to Washington's military forces in the Revolution.

On December 31, 1780, General Benedict Arnold came up the James with his British troops and anchored off Weyanoke. Fortunately, he spared it but burned other nearby plantations.

Young Agnes Harwood of Weyanoke married Fielding Lewis of Gloucester in 1788, and within six years they succeeded to the possession of the waterfront land. Lewis was a promising young man, descended from Colonel Augustine Warner and thus collaterally related to George Washington. This Fielding Lewis—not to be confused with the Fielding Lewis who built Fredericksburg's Kenmore and married Washington's sister—went to William and Mary and served under Lafayette in the Revolution.

Weyanoke was at its happiest during the

Lawrence Lewis, Jr.

Weyanoke on the James near Williamsburg was threatened in the Revolution and the Civil War.

occupancy of Fielding and Agnes Lewis from 1794 to 1834. In 1824 they were visited by Lafayette during his triumphal return to the American colonies, nearly 50 years after he had fought in the Revolution. A family letter describes the French hero's visit en route from Williamsburg to Richmond up the James River.

Fielding Lewis replaced the original Harwood house at Weyanoke with his own larger frame structure, which has been altered but is still standing. The present owner has removed two twentieth-century wings, but left two modern "hyphens" containing needed modern conveniences. The house is a fine example of the Virginia Georgian mansion of the 1790s, three stories high with large chimneys at each corner.

Eleanor Lewis, a daughter of Fielding and Agnes who married Richmond attorney Robert Douthat, inherited Weyanoke from her parents. Fortunately for Douthat, he won $100,000 in an 1821 Pennsylvania lottery and spent $30,000 of

it to buy nearby Westover plantation. When Robert died tragically young in 1828, his widow moved back to Weyanoke to live with her widowed father. Her son, Robert Douthat, Jr., ran Weyanoke after that.

The Civil War and Reconstruction nearly bankrupted the Douthats of Weyanoke. After Robert Douthat died in 1897, the family seat was sold to the wealthy Major Drewry of Westover and to Edmund Saunders of Richmond. From their heirs Lawrence Lewis, Sr. in 1938 bought the house in trust for his son Lawrence, Jr. and his daughter, Mrs. Molly Campbell of Middleburg.

Weyanoke plantation is a proud survival of prosperous farming years on the James, when planters' tobacco ships sailed each fall and spring to Britain, bringing back manufactured goods. It reminds you that Virginia was indeed a dynastic society.

121

34. *Jack Chandler's New Deal*

BY the year 1922 Williamsburg was a diamond in the rough, waiting to be discovered by the world. Things were beginning to look promising, especially after Julian A. C. Chandler in 1919 became president of William and Mary—then a school of about a thousand students. All that was before Rockefeller came along.

Among freshmen arriving in September 1922 was Fred Andrews of Gahanna, Ohio. Not long ago he wrote his 60-year-old recollections, prompted by reading *Cows on the Campus,* my book about pre-Restoration Williamsburg.

His letter gives such an unusual picture that I've asked him to let me reprint it:

> Your book, *Cows on the Campus*, took me down the trail of memory to an early morning in September 1922, when I alighted from the eastbound C&O train in Williamsburg to start my freshman year at the college. Following other ex-passengers on the path across fields and lots, I came to Duke of Gloucester Street. Then I found my way to the room assigned me in Boundary Dormitory No. 1 (newly converted from the Bozarth Hardware warehouse), which was close by Boundary No. 2, newly converted from the Bozarth stable.

My entry into college was in an era which might be titled *Dogs on the Campus*, or, as they were known to students, "The Campus Hounds," a pack of mongrels ranging from 10 to 25 which roamed town and campus. Gentility was added to the pack when the kennel of registered airedales, owned by football coach J. Wilder Tasker, frequently broke loose and joined the mongrels. The amours of members of the pack were never inhibited by the dignity of their surroundings, nor by the presence of coeds.

Memories of town and college include those of English professor John Lesslie Hall's frequently repeated advice . . . to "never look too far up your family tree—you might find a coon sitting on one of the limbs."

I also remember "Booney," the small black janitor and rackboy in Bob Wallace's poolroom, who could put a pool ball in his mouth, and the time "Booney" was unable to remove the ball without Bob Wallace's none-too-gentle assistance. There were those cold Saturdays when rural folk brought to town skinned and cleaned muskrat carcasses for

J. A. C. Chandler stands before the Wren building after becoming college president in 1919.

sale—six on a peeled stick, the sticks being leaned against a utility pole or storefront for display, at 5 cents per carcass or six for 25 cents, which was a worthwhile piece of money at that time.

And then there was "Kitty" Holmes, the college night watchman, whose favorite post was back of the library and who reported couples to Dr. Chandler for reprimand because of exhibiting too much affection while ostensibly searching for books. . . .

I remember Dr. David King, college physician, whose sure cure for malingerers was 2 cc pills, swallowed in his presence, and a throat swabbed with silver nitrate, which left in the mouth for 24 hours a taste like unto the smell of spoiled cabbage.

Mrs. Burgess Luck's boarding house (at Scotland and Boundary) was the finest in the land. . . .

Dr. Chandler often told the story about his classmate who made it through a year of college on a cash outlay of 75 cents. He could have made it on 60 cents but he did like a little chewing tobacco occasionally.

And then there was the story about President Lyon Gardiner Tyler one night asking Doc Billups [the college bellringer] to go out to the sundial in front of the President's House to see what time it was. When Doc protested that it was dark, Dr. Tyler told him to get a lantern and go see anyway.

If J. A. C. Chandler is credited with bringing the college into the 20th century, as he should be, then Beverley Estill Steele should be credited with bringing Jamestown Island into the modern era. Estill Steele was never one to wait for opportunity to knock on his door. . . . At that time Jamestown was divided by a fence into two parts, the APVA reservation and the farm which covered the remainder.

123

William and Mary

The college library early this century also housed portraits and manuscripts.

Roy Ayres presided as caretaker over the APVA reservation and lived in a cottage there. Visitors came principally from occasional excursion boats which tied up at the rickety wharf, whereon passengers would risk life and limb walking to shore. Winder Lane was the tenant on the island farm and having difficulty making his annual rental of $750, despite the great acreage at his disposal.

In the fall of 1923, Beverley Estill Steele, sensing that opportunity might be over the horizon, took the train to Dayton, Ohio, where lived the island's owner, Mrs. Edward Barney. He offered her an annual rental of $1,500 for a 10-year lease plus an option to lease for another 10 years at a rental to be negotiated at the time. This she gladly accepted. . . .

Once in control of the island farm, Estill Steele arranged for a Jamestown ferry [to operate across the James to Surry]. The ferry owners built the slip, rebuilt the island wharf, and replanked the approach for auto traffic. After 1924, Jamestown Island was no longer a dead end for the motorist. Other Steele additions included picnic tables, rental cottages and a "bathhouse" devoid of any plumbing, so that those who went for a swim in the muddy James had to clean up afterwards the best way they could.

During the summer of 1924 I worked on the island and many times I walked the river shore at low tide. Usually I was rewarded by finding a shard [of pottery] or some other relic of the first settlement. These findings were indications that the tides had eaten away the land on which early Jamestown's river-fronting street had been situated and that the foundations still on the island were those of the buildings on another street.

Another indication of what the tides had done in eating away Jamestown Island was the old tree growing in the James River, some 50 to 75 feet from the shore at the lower end of Jamestown Island.

There Fred Andrews's letter ends. Fred transferred from William and Mary to Ohio State University, but he kept in touch with Steele, a prominent Williamsburg businessman, until Steele died.

J. A. C. Chandler created the Sunken Garden on campus before his death in 1934.

William and Mary

Virginia State Library

A major Williamsburg feature before 1953 was the mental hospital on Francis Street.

III.
Comes the Restoration

1926 – 1946

35. *Willie Goodwin's Vision*

TWO graying men in their fifties met on a street corner in Williamsburg in 1926. One was John D. Rockefeller, Jr., who had a great fortune. The other was the Reverend W. A. R. Goodwin, rector of Bruton Parish Church, who had the idea of restoring the town to its eighteenth-century appearance and wanted to tell Mr. Rockefeller about it.

Out of that and other meetings grew the $100,000,000 miracle known as the Williamsburg Restoration. Millions of American have seen it and other millions have heard about this fabulous village that, in the span of a few years, turned back time two centuries. Relatively few people know the story of the man who dreamed of a long dead colonial capital brought back to life—and who, before he died, saw his dream come true.

"How did you ever think of such a thing?" townsmen and tourists used to ask the doctor when the transformation was just beginning.

His answer was to lift from its shelf a large, faded book—the title, *Hidden Cities Restored.* Many years before, when Willie Goodwin was a boy on his father's farm in Nelson County, Virginia, he had bought that book with his first earnings. When he went off to school at

Roanoke College, and later at the Virginia Theological Seminary at Alexandria, he had kept it to read and to muse over as he watched, in the years after the Civil War, the decay of so many old buildings through which Virginia's history had moved.

Bruton Parish, to which the Reverend Mr. Goodwin came early in his ministry, gave him his first opportunity as a practical restorer. He was a poor young rector and Williamsburg, lingering on as a small country town since it had ceased to be Virginia's seat of government, was not rich. Nevertheless, he started a one-man campaign to restore the church, collecting money from parishioners and any others he could get at. At night he combed town and church records for information about the structure as it used to be. With the money and knowledge thus acquired, he restored Bruton to its colonial appearance.

On the 300th anniversary of the establishment of the Episcopal Church in America, in 1907, the restored church was rededicated. The rector stood at the lectern, given by President Theodore Roosevelt, to read the lessons from the Bible presented by King Edward VII of England and delivered in person by the Lord

William and Mary, C. E. Cheyne, Hampton

Dr. Goodwin partly restored Bruton in 1907 for Jamestown's 300th anniversary.

Bishop of London, who was in attendance.

Some 30 years later, when Dr. Goodwin lay smoking his pipe, calmly facing the end then close at hand, a stranger who had been admitted to see him remarked, "Every time I hear of this town, I think of a letter I got from a young preacher here when I was a young fellow working in Norfolk. He said they were restoring the church where my ancestors had worshipped, and he thought I ought to help. I don't know why I did it—I was poor as a churchmouse—but I sent him ten dollars."

Others by the bedside laughed—they recognized the technique. Dr. Goodwin smiled. "You are a brave man to come here right now," he said, "I was only a young preacher then, but I am older now and I have learned a lot. Bruton is being restored over again—and you are older, too. Perhaps you can afford a larger gift this time."

The vestry of St. Paul's Church in Rochester, New York, heard of Dr. Goodwin's work, and, in 1908, invited him to take charge there. "Pre-

posterous," exploded elderly Bruton parishioners. Dr. Goodwin thought otherwise. He had done all he could for Williamsburg for the time being and looked forward to a larger sphere. The good folk of Bruton will tell you how they settled back confidently waiting to hear Dr. Goodwin way up north holler "Enough!" He never did. Under his ministry, St. Paul's became one of the outstanding parishes in western New York, with a congregation of 1,200 and a system of weekday religious instruction that was widely copied.

Time passed and Williamsburg began to forget Bruton's restorer. Then in 1919 Julian A. C. Chandler became president of the College of William and Mary. Like all else in Williamsburg, the college was poor and struggling, but Dr. Chandler was determined to revitalize the institution and give it standing comparable to its age—second only to Harvard's in this country. Would Dr. Goodwin come back to Williamsburg to help? Dr. Goodwin would. And

129

back he came in 1923 to become director of endowment and professor of biblical literature and religious education at William and Mary.

As a representative of the college he went to New York in 1924 to speak at a dinner given by the united chapters of Phi Beta Kappa. John D. Rockefeller, Jr. was present. Dr. Goodwin talked to Mr. Rockefeller and invited him to come to Williamsburg.

Two years passed before Mr. Rockefeller actually came. But when he drove in one morning from Hampton, Dr. Goodwin, forewarned, was waiting at the edge of town for the Rockefeller family. Up and down Duke of Gloucester Street and through endless side streets the rector led the Rockefellers on a walking tour of discovery. At that time 88 colonial dwellings remained standing within the limits of the old town, and it was Dr. Goodwin's hope that the man who had restored Rheims Cathedral and the palace and gardens of Versailles would buy this area and restore these buildings—and possibly, as well, some that had disappeared.

Money wasn't mentioned. Dr. Goodwin gave his prospect time to think over what he had seen, while he, himself, cast about for an opportunity to drive home the appeal. At that point he sought the advice of James Hardy Dillard, rector of the William and Mary board of visitors and a member of the Rockefeller-endowed General Education Board. Dr. Dillard in turn spoke to Colonel Arthur Woods, Mr. Rockefeller's adviser, and in November 1926, the financier made his second trip to Williamsburg—to see the Phi Beta Kappa Hall dedicated at the college and to talk to Dr. Goodwin.

Admittedly, Mr. Rockefeller was interested. The project appealed to him, he wrote later, because "Williamsburg . . . offered an opportunity to restore a complete area and free it entirely from alien or inharmonious surroundings as well as to preserve the beauty and charm of the old buildings and gardens of the city and its historic significance." When he left he authorized Dr. Goodwin, confidentially, to have drawings prepared of the town and plans drafted for a

renovation of the Wren Building at William and Mary. He made it clear that he was not committed to pay for either enterprise.

For the drawings and plans Dr. Goodwin went to William G. Perry of the firm of Perry, Shaw & Hepburn, Boston architects. Some time before, Mr. Perry, then a stranger, had passed the George Wythe House which Dr. Goodwin was restoring for use as a parish house. A detail of the door moldings had the doctor stumped, and work was at a standstill. The visitor pointed out the cause of the trouble and offered to send from Boston antique locks and keys for the house. The doctor remembered that, and Mr. Perry got the Williamsburg job. But even to him the purpose of the survey and the name of the backer remained a secret.

In the darkness of a winter night, after the unsuspecting Williamsburgers had long gone to bed, Mr. Perry and two assistants took measurements of the streets and buildings with a tapeline. No one witnessed this strange procedure, Dr. Goodwin used to say, except a drunken workman, reeling home shortly before dawn.

Preliminary sketches were first shown to Mr. Rockefeller in Williamsburg. Six months later in a suite in the Vanderbilt Hotel in New York the maps and sketches were propped against the walls and Mr. Rockefeller entered with his associates—Colonel Woods, Charles O. Heydt, his adviser on real estate, and Thomas M. Debevoise, his attorney. From time to time Dr. Goodwin would leave the conference to telephone Mr. Perry, cloistered on another floor of the hotel, nervously waiting. At 9 o'clock that night Mr. Perry was standing by at a club, as instructed, when Dr. Goodwin entered with a stranger whose appearance was familiar—John D. Rockefeller, Jr. The secret was out. Mr. Rockefeller would restore Williamsburg.

Before working plans could be completed, however, the owner of one of the principal buildings on Duke of Gloucester Street died, and the house was offered for sale. Dr. Goodwin wired Mr. Rockefeller for advice. Back came the answer: buy the Ludwell-Paradise House without revealing the identity of his backer. The signature was "David's Father," which, shortened to "Mr. David," remained Mr. Rockefeller's pseudonym during the secret negotiations.

Before long Dr. Goodwin held title to property up and down Duke of Gloucester Street, and Williamsburg was buzzing with excitement. How could a poor clergyman buy land, people asked. Some thought he was agent for Henry Ford, who just then was assembling Greenfield Village at Dearborn, Michigan. Others suspected a tie-in with George Eastman because Dr. Goodwin had known the camera manufacturer in Rochester.

The rector of Bruton Parish laughed his questioners off. But property owners knew something was afoot, and prices for tumbledown houses and vacant lots began to skyrocket. When the time came for the town of Williamsburg to transfer public land to the Restoration, Dr Goodwin found himself balked for the first time by a law which forbade the town to convey property to unknown persons. He called a town meeting in June 1928, and told his secret.

"Williamsburg is rich in historic buildings and memories which for many years it has been our desire to preserve," he said to the eager townspeople gathered in the high school auditorium. "Both in its historical associations and in its relics the town lends itself to a complete restoration. About a year ago Mr. John D. Rockefeller, Jr. came to Williamsburg. . . ."

The community was electrified by the news. A balladeer in the local *Virginia Gazette* lamented, "My gosh, they've sold the town," but he was reassured by others less apprehensive. A Greek restaurateur whose land had been bought sent Dr. Goodwin a turkey with celery dressing and a box of cigars, accompanied by a note reading, "Thanking you for your cooperation in the work which you are doing." ("The only commission I ever got in my life," laughed Dr. Goodwin.) Mr. Rockefeller himself contributed to the merriment when he told a local audience, "I'd heard of people being taken for a ride. Dr. Goodwin took *me* for a walk."

Once the Restoration came out into the open, the work sped forward. A research organization was created to comb America and the British Isles for records needed for the undertaking. In

Dr. W. A. R. Goodwin greeted President and Mrs. Roosevelt at Bruton Church.

Mary Goodwin collection

the years that the Restoration has been at work, it has razed or removed nearly 600 buildings of fairly modern vintage from the Historic Area, restored or repaired 88 old buildings still standing, and reconstructed others from the records which the researchers produced.

What used to be a faded Virginia village became an American shrine of gleaming clapboard and mellow brick. The Williamsburg tourist roster shows that more than a million visitors see it each year. Its spiritual and cultural influence is widespread, and artists recognize "the Williamsburg motif" as one of the most important in architecture and decoration. Even more notable is the effect in making Americans conscious of their history. That was what Dr. Goodwin hoped and predicted.

The doctor remained at the helm of the Restoration until the course was charted, but gradually others began to share the task which he had undertaken. Although only 62, he was beginning to feel the effects of overwork and he still had his duties at Bruton, for he had resumed the rectorate in 1926. A heart ailment developed in 1931 after he had spent a year organizing a celebration commemorating the 150th anniversary of the American victory at Yorktown. Physicians who took X-rays told him his heart muscles were those of a man 90.

This was no wonder to members of his family, for Dr. Goodwin for years had done the work of four ordinary men. He was minister, architect, scholar, and businessman, and he played the three added roles without sacrificing his ministerial effectiveness. To his parishioners he was the most understanding of clerics, typified by his pipe and his baggy tweed suit. He was, he said, neither a high churchman nor a low churchman but a "broad" churchman. As amateur architect he won the respect of the highly trained members of that profession who took up the work he began in Williamsburg. As scholar he was thorough and assiduous, though he had a disquieting habit of misquoting poetry, which he said "improved" it. As a businessman he was a marvel to behold.

Characteristic is the story he himself used to tell of how he got a new steeple for Bruton by showing a northern industrialist and his wife through the churchyard. They came to the bell tower. "I'm ashamed of its appearance—the cornice has rotted," Dr. Goodwin said deprecatingly. The tycoon scowled. "That looks like hell." Then in embarrassment he begged the doctor's pardon. "That's all right," Dr. Goodwin reassured him. "Every man is entitled to his own opinion if he will back it up. The contractors say it will cost just $1,200 to repair the tower." The tycoon paid it.

Once in New York Dr. Goodwin called on an insurance executive and with characteristic earnestness described the need for funds for work in Williamsburg. The official got a chance at last to say he had made all the commitments he could afford. "I haven't asked you for a cent, sir," said Dr. Goodwin. "You mistake me. All I want is a letter of introduction to Mr. _____," a wealthy international banker. Half an hour later that letter got Dr. Goodwin into the office of one of New York's businessmen. He emerged with $15,000 for his project.

He did not retire until October 1938, when life was ebbing away so fast that he could feel it go. At home in an oxygen tent he battled his illness, emerging whenever he could to confer with his associates from the church and the Restoration and to dictate letters and reminiscences.

He died just before midnight on September 7, 1939, and two days later he was buried beside the door of his pulpit in the aisle of his beloved Bruton, while the old bell in the church tower clanged dolorously. The highbacked pews recalling those in which Washington and Jefferson once had worshipped were lined now with churchmen, philanthropists, parishioners come to listen to the last words of tribute to "The Doctor." But the truest record of his good works lay outside, where a midday sun shone on a gleaming village that had been raised from the dead by a generous man with a great fortune and by his friend, who had a vision.

36. *John and Abby Rockefeller*

THE year was 1926. In Williamsburg a pale March sunshine covered the gnarled mulberry trees and brought blue and yellow crocus into flower on Duke of Gloucester Street.

Near Bassett Hall, an old white house at one end of town, the Reverend William Archer Rutherfoord Goodwin stood and waited beside the road from Hampton. Suddenly, a black Lincoln touring car bearing Mr. and Mrs. John D. Rockefeller, Jr. and three of their six children drove up beside Dr. Goodwin and stopped. It was Easter vacation for school-age Winthrop, Laurance, and David Rockefeller and their parents had brought them to Virginia. At the invitation of the preacher, they'd come to see Williamsburg.

It was the beginning of a visit that was to change Williamsburg. More than that, it was the beginning of a 30-year love affair between Williamsburg's people and their new neighbors, the quiet heir to the Standard Oil millions and his first wife, the sparkling Abby Aldrich Rockefeller.

"The Rockefellers act like Virginians, but the Virginians try to act like Rockefellers," reported one paper. But Williamsburg's awe gradually changed to ease in company of the quiet couple who came to spend a few months each year in their town.

In those first years the Rockefellers, like everybody else, stayed at Jack Spencer's cozy Colonial Inn and then in rooms of the newly reconstructed Raleigh Tavern. One day Abby Rockefeller delightedly told her friends, "John has promised we can live at Bassett Hall, and we won't even have to take in tourists!"

As workmen removed Victorian false fronts which hid colonial houses and taverns, Mr. Rockefeller often stood and watched, unrecognized by passers-by. Sometimes he asked a question. A carpenter told the curious stranger, "I wouldn't be surprised even if Mr. Rockefeller himself should drop in on the job." The stranger chuckled, for he was John Rockefeller, Jr.

Though the philanthropist at first agreed to pay for the restoration only of William and Mary's Wren Building and a few other major structures, he warmed to the project with each visit. Research kept turning up discoveries which excited his interest. A Revolutionary War billeting map, made by French engineers about 1782, showed every building then in town. An unknown copper plate in the Bodleian Library at Oxford provided structural details of the Wren Building, Capitol, and Governor's Palace.

A manuscript sketch by Thomas Jefferson showed the ground plan of the Governor's Palace as it was when he lived there as Virginia's Revolutionary governor in 1779 and 1780.

"Mr. Rockefeller would have made a good architect," said one of the project's first administrators. "He has a keen eye for proportion, space, and detail." In meetings with his staff he asked questions and made suggestions which often improved their plans. He was a stickler for accuracy and authenticity.

When one building was half complete, new evidence showed it to be a few feet off its correct site. What to do? "Tear it down and build it in the right place," said the man who was paying for it.

When the Randolph family's handsome Tazewell Hall was found to have been moved from its original location about 1906 to make way for a street, Mr. Rockefeller insisted that it be moved away. He wanted each building to be on its original location, and Tazewell Hall could not be.

During the Rockefeller years, Abby Rockefeller was collecting early American paintings and sculpture. She had a keen interest in the research and furnishing of the interiors, delighting in the rediscovery of Williamsburg's original wall colors and furnishings. At Bassett Hall, she decorated the walls with primitive paintings, which she later gave to Colonial Williamsburg. Displayed for years in the Ludwell-Paradise House, the collection in 1957 was installed in a museum of its own. The Abby Aldrich Rockefeller Folk Art Collection is today a growing center for the increasingly popular study of naïve art forms.

To make life easier for owners of historic houses which Colonial Williamsburg bought, they were often permitted to occupy them for life. Though life tenants were obliged to make their own minor repairs, Mr. Rockefeller discreetly had steps repaired and railings put up for elderly ones who could ill afford it.

The Rockefellers were amused by the amiable eccentricities of some new neighbors. Calling on the bearded patrician, Peyton Randolph Nelson, they were greeted by an Old Testament apparition in white undershirt and dungarees, leaning on a shepherd's crook. "Welcome to the bon ton section of Williamsburg," cried the old man on his sagging front steps. The visitors found the interior littered with firewood and ashes.

Once he had sold his Tazewell Hall to the restoration, Peyton Nelson let the house fall into utter disrepair. Since his deed of sale made the restoration responsible for major repairs, he said, "I just let minor repairs grow into major repairs."

Townspeople reciprocated Rockefeller kindnesses with preserves, wild game, and other local fare. One fisherman took to Bassett Hall a striped bass he had hooked. Mr. Rockefeller thanked him warmly, then added with a half smile, "You know, people don't often give *me* things."

Brought up a Baptist, Mr. Rockefeller neither drank nor played cards. He and his wife entertained simply, usually at six o'clock dinner and the movies. The usher at the local theater saved a few back-row seats when the Rockefellers were in town. Afterward, the host and hostess often sent their guests home in their car while they themselves walked back to Bassett Hall.

Walking or driving—usually a Model A Ford in the early Williamsburg years—were favorite Rockefeller pastimes. "We look in the windows, and we look at the moon and the stars," he explained to an interviewer who asked about his nightly walks. "You can't appreciate Williamsburg unless you walk through the town. Always you see something different: a fence or a chimney from some angle you never saw before."

Sometimes Abby Rockefeller packed a picnic and the two drove up the plantation road along the James River. On each outing they chose a different side road, stopping at lunch time near the river's edge to open their picnic basket. Sometimes they sat on the grass and sometimes on the running board. They delighted in the colors and moods of the seasons.

At Bassett Hall, the garden and woods were their pride, and they and their guests walked there almost daily when in residence. From his European travels, he knew how neatly kept were European forests. Unhappy to see fallen trees and underbrush along the Colonial Parkway to Jamestown and Yorktown, he asked National Park Service officials how much it would cost to remove such debris. Then he wrote a check for it, insisting on no publicity. At Jamestown, he gave money for an eight-mile wilderness trail for hikers and automobilists around the island.

Each Sunday they were in Williamsburg, the Rockefellers went to church. They alternated between the Baptist, Episcopal, Methodist, and Presbyterian, for they were increasingly interdenominational in outlook. At the Methodist service one Sunday, usher Archie Brooks, who was taking up the offering, saw a gray-haired stranger drop a $20 bill into the plate. The usher stopped, leaned over, and whispered to the stranger, "Sir, didn't you make a mistake?"

Brought up as the son of "America's wealthiest man," John Rockefeller Jr. always shunned the limelight. His instinct for privacy was reinforced by the advice of his business advisor, Frederick T. Gates: "In this business [of philanthropy] you have to lead the life of a recluse. Never make friends. Don't join clubs. Avoid knowing people intimately." But none of this was necessary in unspoiled Tidewater Virginia. "I feel I really belong in Williamsburg," the philanthropist said in a rare show of zeal in 1941.

He enjoyed the lack of ostentation, ceremony, and formality. "Most people are willing to let you be just folks," he said. "That's the way we always have been—perfectly plain and homey, and most people treat us the same way. When Mrs. Rockefeller and I were first married, I taught a men's Bible class and almost every Sunday we would have some of the members in for dinner."

He paused while strollers passed on Duke of Gloucester Street. "Sunday Mrs. Rockefeller and I sat in front of the postoffice for a long

Colonial Williamsburg

Abby and John D. Rockefeller, Jr. oversaw the Restoration in their lifetime.

time and watched the people passing by. We often do that. Of course, your Southern charm and hospitality have meant very much. You Southerners express so graciously what the people of the North may feel just as strongly but don't show."

Often when Mr. Rockefeller lunched with advisers and architects, his wife entertained ladies at Bassett Hall or lunched in town. Arriving for tea one day at the Tucker-Coleman House, she found Mrs. George Preston Coleman, the mayor's wife, putting out a chimney fire. "How exciting," Abby Rockefeller said, rushing to her aid. "I do love a fire!"

Unable to eat lunch one day at a party in her honor, she asked her hostess if she might pass her plate for other guests to divide. "John would be disappointed if he knew I wasted food," she explained.

Having served in girlhood as hostess for her father, Senator Nelson Aldrich of Rhode Island, Abby Rockefeller was at ease in any situation. Her vivacity and humor enlivened the Rockefeller household and charmed her reserved husband. Writing to a son after persuading Mr. Rockefeller to see the stage play, "Harvey," she reported that "Your father enjoyed it, but he asked me if it 'proved anything.' I told him it proved the importance of having pleasant people in the world. Though the principal character was a drunkard, he was so very delightful that you had the feeling all the time that perhaps to be pleasant and amusing might be more important than to be sober and disagreeable."

When the United States entered World War II, four Rockefeller sons entered military service while the fifth, Nelson, served on missions for the State Department. After that, Abby and John D. often came to Williamsburg without them, though they occasionally invited servicemen from nearby bases to fill the empty chairs at Bassett Hall's dinner table. On Thanksgiving in 1941 they had ten soldiers from Fort Eustis for dinner. "We got two for one," Mr. Rockefeller quipped.

Williamsburg's restorer wanted soldiers and sailors to visit the town, for he felt that it might teach them history and encourage patriotism. As the motto for the project he chose "That the Future May Learn from the Past." He saw the experiences of 1776 as a guide. "We always can learn from great men," he said. "We always need great leaders. The men of colonial Williamsburg were individuals. They had the courage to be themselves and to do what they thought was right." Much as he admired the town's beauty, it was its history which touched him most deeply.

After Abby Rockefeller died in 1948, Mr. Rockefeller in 1951 married the widow of a college classmate, Martha Baird Allen, of Providence. By that time he was 77 and his visits to Williamsburg were fewer, but he was present in 1957 for the opening of the museum housing Abby's folk art collection.

On his 85th birthday in 1959, Williamsburg friends deluged him with birthday cards. A year later he died, and hundreds of his friends gathered at Bassett Hall to memorialize him. Together they sang some of the hymns that he had so often joined in when he and his family had first "discovered" Williamsburg with the Reverend Mr. Goodwin. The town that in 1926 had almost succumbed to blight and decay now shone again in its eighteenth-century beauty.

The influence of "Mister Junior" as his staff called him, lived on in Williamsburg after his death. True to the principles of its founder, Colonial Williamsburg pioneered in lifting racial restrictions among its employes and its millions of visitors. When the Supreme Court outlawed segregation in public schools, Williamsburg and its adjoining county complied with little fuss. And when "dry" Virginia in the 1950s relaxed its laws against the serving of wine and beer, Mr. Rockefller readily accepted the change in Colonial Williamsburg's restaurants, though he remained a teetotaller.

Perhaps what Williamsburgers admired most in Mr. Rockefeller was his devotion to principle during years of great change. They liked his simplicity, his candor, his family-mindedness, his thoughtfulness, his distaste for show, his evident Christian faith. They shared his Victorian values and his old-fashioned idealism. Though Virginians had never been as austere as their New England contemporaries, they respected Mr. Rockefeller as one of the last puritans of his age.

As it enters its second half-century, the Restoration which Mr. Rockefeller and Dr. Goodwin launched faces more changes. For one thing, it has grown from a rich man's project into a treasured national resource. Since Winthrop Rockefeller's death in 1973, the chairmanship of the foundation's board has gone outside the family. Increasingly, Colonial Williamsburg sees its support coming from diverse sources across the land. Already it has received unique collections of furniture, porcelain, and other antiquities, and it seeks more.

It has recently added a national resource collection of the decorative arts and expanded its scholarly thrust in several directions. Said Chairman Carlisle Humelsine, "We must find ways to improve our activities in the decorative arts, in archaeology, in folk art, at Carter's Grove, and in other areas." It sees itself a center of research and preservation, in co-operation with the College of William and Mary and other agencies in the Jamestown-Williamsburg-Yorktown triangle.

Would "Mister Junior" object to the decline of Rockefeller influence in the foundation he created? The answer reflects his familiar modesty. "It doesn't matter who does a thing," he said near the end of his life. "The achievement is what matters. If something is noble and fine, it doesn't make any difference whether the man who did it is Smith or Jones or Brown, if you're lucky enough to be any of them. The doer is not important, either to the public or himself."

Even so, Williamsburg won't soon forget the rare couple who came into its life some 60 years ago. They are as much a part of its history now as Washington, Jefferson, or Patrick Henry.

37. *Williamsburg and the Model T*

EVERYBODY who grew up in Tidewater in the 1920s and 30s came at some time to see Williamsburg. It provided a Sunday objective for your family's new Model T (or Durant, or Huppmobile), for gas was less than 25 cents a gallon. The road through the Peninsula had been hard-surfaced by the Army in World War I to expedite troop movements, and the macadam was reasonably bumpless if you went slowly.

Who can forget his first view of unrestored Duke of Gloucester divided into two car lanes by a platoon of telephone poles and street lights? What was more romantic than those gnarled mulberries and unpainted old houses, Victorianized to look like western saloons in Tom Mix movies? Farm wagons abounded in the town then, drawn by horses or oxen. Henri Mouquin, a retired New York restaurateur, occasionally drove in from his York County farm in his coach with matching horses.

From Newport News to Williamsburg was an hour trip at 25 mph. It made an easy afternoon drive. After church and a big Sunday dinner—an immoveable feast in those days—my family would set out for the trip. The narrow road curled through Hilton, Goalder's Store, Morri-

son, and the waterworks. Then came Lee Hall and Grove, a village which grew up outside the Carter's Grove entrance. Billboards were everywhere. The First National Bank of Newport News proclaimed itself "Home of Mr. 4 Percent," with a picture of him. Whatever happened to that guy?

The highway ran down Duke of Gloucester Street before branching at College Corner into Richmond and Jamestown roads. You couldn't avoid Williamsburg if you wanted to. But who'd want to miss the Asylum, as we called Eastern State then, with inmates lounging against its fence to wave and yell to passers-by? And of course you had to see the college, which had recently scandalized folk by admitting women. Men and women studying biology together? And physiology? And physical education?

I can remember cows grazing the Williamsburg greens, keeping the grass mowed. I didn't know it then, but some of them were owned by an eccentric ex-cowboy and gold-miner, Peyton Randolph Nelson, who lived at Tazewell Hall on the site of the present Williamsburg Lodge. Peyton Nelson was proud of his blue-blooded Jerseys. "They're from the Lee herd," he said, implying they were not to be touched by ordi-

Colonial Williamsburg

Early autos lined Duke of Gloucester Street near College Corner in 1928.

nary hands. When he suspected that they were being milked by unknown hands, he put brassieres on his cows.

At College Corner, the principal attraction was Bob Wallace's College Shop. Jocks in sweaters and high-water pants lounged outside, whistling at girls. Bob had come from Fox Hill to become a three-star William and Mary athlete, staying on in town to make a fortune. His shop was both bus depot, soda fountain, souvenir shop, and hash house. Big Bob was usually there, glad-handing in a gravel voice and listening to the music of his cash register.

Halfway down the street was the town's main hostelry, the Colonial Inn. It sat where Chowning's Tavern now is, a rambling building with a wide porch and a cream-colored lounge, carpeted in wine red, which was then thought by Virginians to be authentic colonial decor. Ellen Glasgow came down from Richmond now and then to stay there.

Greyhound buses would stop at the inn if you asked the driver to do so. That worked well for those of us who could get free passes on the Peninsula Greyhound bus, then a locally-owned franchise, to ride to Williamsburg on Sunday afternoon and come back on the next bus.

As cars increased, Charles Person opened a

Virginia Historical Society

The Courthouse of 1770 and the Colonial Inn lined Duke of Gloucester in the 1920s.

garage and Ford agency on Duke of Gloucester. When sold by his late son Billy in the 1970s, it was the oldest Ford dealership in Virginia in the same family. A rival garage, housed in an ugly metal shop, called itself the "Toot-And-Come-In," after the recent 1921 discovery in Egypt of the tomb of Tut-Ankh-Amen.

When I first knew Williamsburg, the Wren Building was called "the Main Building." Earlier it had simply been called "the College" for lack of other academic structures. It was J. A. C. Chandler, the college's head after 1919, who named it for Christopher Wren, who had designed it or inspired its design. Chandler had the college librarian Earl G. Swem, write to England to establish Wren's connection, but it's still uncertain.

Bruton Church also attracted my family and other motorists. Across the street from Bruton, men of the Pulaski Club sat on benches and talked endlessly.

The sight of coeds at the college in the 1920s excited interest. They were a curiosity. People called them "Marys" and the men "Williams," but that didn't stick, fortunately. The girls were heavily restricted until the 1950s, after World War II revolutionized things.

Except for Henry Dennison Cole's postcard shop across the street from Bruton, few Williamsburgers realized the money to be made from souvenirs. The biggest operator was wily, talkative Charles Evans Hughes, who ran Hughes' Hotel at Providence Forge, with a gas station full of junk souvenirs and fine Wedgewood pottery. I coveted a large colored porcelain lobster, lettered "Souvenir of Salt Lake City," but I couldn't afford it.

If my family had time, we'd ride out to Norge for five-cent ice cream cones at Mrs. Smith's. Her little building is still there, weed-grown and deserted on the edge of Norge. It was a worthy forerunner of Howard Johnson's, High's, and Baskin-Robbins. The ice cream melted fast, but if you slurped ravenously, you could beat the law of gravity.

Williamsburg was a seedy place, but it had

140

that romance that Ruskin wrote about. Thanks to the college coeds, it was full of life. It had many educated families and well-known figures. John Garland Pollard was teaching at the college before his election as governor in 1930. Ashton Dovell was powerful in politics, and Judge Frank Armistead, Channing Hall and Bat Peachy were lawyers. George Preston Coleman was mayor, and Charles Person, R. B. Watts, Will Bozarth, and Alec Harwood were leading businessmen.

Two other memorable figures were Henry Billups, the college sexton, and Alec Pleasants, who kept the Powder Horn for the APVA. Both were black.

Being halfway between the James and York, Williamsburg seemed to us port-dwellers to be hotter than we in summer. I doubt that it is, really, but certainly it draws some of the most violent thunderstorms I've ever witnessed. On one August Sunday in the 1920s, when our Model T was nosing down Duke of Gloucester, lightning struck the road near the Powder Magazine just ahead of us.

Years later, Episcopal Bishop George Gunn of Norfolk told me that he and Bishop William A. Brown had witnessed a similar stroke near the same place. Gunn, then a young clergyman, asked his bishop "to offer some words of thanksgiving," as he put it. "Whew, George, that was too damn close for comfort," replied the feisty old bishop, mopping his brow.

Thunder and lightning still rage at Devilsburg, as Jefferson called it, but those dear souls who graced the town in the '20s are now beyond its reach. They passed on to us a glorious unique heritage. Let thunder and lightning do their worst.

Colonial Inn on Chowning's Duke of Gloucester site was a pre-Restoration hostelry.

Colonial Williamsburg

38. *Abby Rockefeller's Contribution*

ABBY Aldrich Rockefeller was a remarkable woman. In Williamsburg, where she spent several months each year from the late 1920s until she died in 1948, the tall New Englander's memory is kept alive by the Abby Aldrich Folk Art Collection and by Bassett Hall, a clapboard house on Francis Street that she filled with her personality. When it was opened to the public in 1980, a *New York Times* writer called it "down-right homey and full of the sort of exuberant mix of furnishings that curators abhor but people adore." It conveys the warm, colorful spirit of Abby Rockefeller.

That was the smiling, white-haired woman Williamsburg remembers: spontaneous and completely herself. Its rooms convey her love for beauty. They also reveal her zeal for the crafts and folk paintings of early America, epitomized in the collection of eighteenth- and nineteenth-century folk art she amassed and gave to Williamsburg before she died. The collection forms the core of the museum named for her by her family in 1957.

At first, most people saw little merit in the "primitive" paintings she acquired. In those days, her husband told a reporter at Bassett

Hall, "Some people don't care for this amateur art and don't see any reason for having it because it isn't great art, but it looks right in a setting like this because these are the very pictures people would have hung on their walls at this period." However, folk art is widely appreciated today, and the collection in Williamsburg is much visited.

Abby Rockefeller furnished the pre-1766 Bassett Hall with eighteenth- and nineteenth-century American furniture in Chippendale, Federal, and Empire styles. Rugs range from Oriental to Aubusson and draperies go from the simple to the elaborate. The house is a mixture of American, European, and Oriental objects that reflect its owners' tastes.

However, it is Mrs. Rockefeller's folk art that chiefly distinguishes Bassett Hall's furnishings. As a founder of New York City's Museum of Modern Art, she felt that American primitive or naïve paintings were forerunners of the American school of painting in the 1930s and 40s. She was one of the major collectors of such primitives.

Mrs. Rockefeller began collecting folk art in 1929. Her husband had given the go-ahead for the restoration of Williamsburg three years earlier,

Author's collection

The Rockefellers: Laurance, Babs, John 3rd, Abby and David, Winthrop, John, Jr., and Nelson

and both were absorbed in it. In 1935 she loaned several hundred pieces of her folk art for exhibit in the Ludwell-Paradise House on Duke of Gloucester, the first building acquired by her husband in 1926 for restoration. She gave most of her folk art to Colonial Williamsburg in 1939.

The collection by 1957 numbered 424 paintings and sculptures by early artists or craftsmen. Most of the artists were self-taught amateurs, some of them unknown, who often were house painters, carpenters, or cabinetmakers. Some, like Edward Hicks of Pennsylvania, whose Biblical scene "The Peaceable Kingdom" was duplicated for many patrons, have become famous. Others were early Germanic immigrants to Virginia and other colonies, who penned fraktur drawings or decorated wooden furniture with stylized tulips and roses.

Other folk art collections were being assembled in the same era by Edith Gregor Halpert of New York, Maxim Karolik of Newport, Rhode Island, and by Edgar and Bernice Chrysler Garbisch of Maryland. Some of the Garbisch collection was acquired on their deaths by Walter Chrysler, Jr., Mrs. Garbisch's brother, and is in the Chrysler Museum in Norfolk.

When Mr. Rockefeller left the house and furnishings on his death to John D. Rockefeller 3rd,

Frank Dementi photo: Colonial Williamsburg

Abby and John D. Rockefeller, Jr. welcomed World War II servicemen to Williamsburg.

the inheritor and his wife Blanchette kept the furnishings largely unchanged. He was Colonial Williamsburg's chairman from 1939 to 1953. After his death in an automobile accident in 1978, his widow gave the house and its furnishings to Colonial Williamsburg, along with 585 acres of grounds and woodlands. Both gifts were valued at more than five million dollars.

Bassett Hall stands off Francis Street, in sight of the colonial Capitol. Built just before the Revolution, it got its name when owned after 1800 by Burwell Bassett, a nephew of Martha Washington. A guest of Bassett's was Irish poet Thomas Moore, who wrote "To a Firefly" there in 1804 after seeing lightning bugs in the garden. A later owner was Abel Upshur, Secretary of State in 1843–44 under his Williamsburg neighbor, President John Tyler.

In the Rockefeller years, they entertained world figures, including Prime Minister

Mackenzie King of Canada, King Paul and Queen Frederika of Greece, Queen Mother Elizabeth of England, Emperor Hirohito, and President Lyndon Johnson. When the house was opened to the public in 1980, a garage was converted to a reception building with pho-tographs of Rockefellers and Aldriches.

Today John D., Jr. and Abby Rockefeller are recognized as two of America's important tastemakers of the twentieth century. Bassett Hall is the most personal of their legacies to a town inseparably linked to their lives.

The Wren Building was unrestored when Rockefellers visited College Corner in 1926

Colonial Williamsburg

39. *The Morecock Sisters*

WHEN the decision to restore Williamsburg reached the press in 1928, some oldtimers wailed that the town would be ruined. Among them were four sisters—"the Morecock girls"—who lived in the Benjamin Waller House and were active in town life. Ironically, the Waller House and Bassett Hall are adjoining properties, so the sisters unavoidably became neighbors and eventually good friends of the Rockefellers.

Though gone now for 30 years, the four spinsters of Francis Street are alive in spirit. "No family here was more attractive or beloved," says Dr. Janet Kimbrough of the Tucker House, a life resident. Their names are often mentioned in Williamsburg.

When I moved to town in 1951, I heard frequent mention of "Miss Pinkie," "Miss Agnes," and "Miss Kitty." Alas, Pinkie (christened Elizabeth but nicknamed for her rosy cheeks) died in 1954. Already dead since 1939 was Patty (Mary Ann), the intellectual sister, who had been secretary to President Lyon Tyler of William and Mary. He called her "Hattie-Pattie-Boomelattie." The other two sisters followed in 1957.

Today the Morecock line is carried on by great-nieces and great-nephews—grandchildren of the Morecocks' only brother, Edloe, who was Collector of Customs in Newport News for 30 years before he died in 1929. "Why did attractive women like the Morecocks stay single?" I asked an old Williamsburger. "Because their mother was too possessive to let them go," she told me. "Nobody was good enough for her daughters."

Whatever the reason, "the girls" had plenty of admirers. One bachelor, Moses Harrell, a friend of their father, left the Waller house to Pinkie, the prettiest sister, in his will. Another of Pinkie's admirers was Hugh Cumming of Hampton, who became Surgeon General of the United States many years ago.

Among Miss Kitty's beaux were two William and Mary students who went on to the University of Virginia. One was John Lloyd Newcomb, who became its president, and the other Oscar Ferguson, who became its dean.

Agnes, known as "Ag" or "Aggie," was pursued by Jennings Hobson, who became an Episcopal minister. She was very popular with boys whom she taught mandolin and guitar. An old photo shows her surrounded by strummers.

Colonial Williamsburg

Pinky Morecock gathers her students in the backyard of the Bland-Wetherburn house.

"All the sisters were musical," recalled Mrs. Mildred Morecock Kauffmann of Charlottesville, a niece. "They were goodlooking, bright, loved poetry, and were full of fun. We children doted on them."

The Morecocks' father, William Henry Edloe Morecock, had moved to town from New Kent after the Civil War to become a lawyer and clerk of court. He and his wife had eight children, three dying early. When out-of-town lawyers came to attend court, Clerk Morecock always invited three or four home for lunch.

"They always came," Kitty recalled. "We were told, 'Now, so-and-so is going to be here, and you must have on your company manners."

The Morecocks grew up in Wetherburn's Tavern on Duke of Gloucester Street, then called the Richard Bland House. After their father died in 1896 and Pinkie inherited the Benjamin Waller house, Mrs. Morecock and her daughters moved there to spend their lives. The house is now restored to its eighteenth-century state.

While growing up in Wetherburn's, the

Colonial Williamsburg

Mrs. Edloe Morecock, right, on Francis Street with a daughter in a nineteenth-century photo.

Morecocks went to private schools. Like most Williamsburg girls of their day, they did not attend college. Then all went to work in town. Kitty started the Richard Bland Tea Room at her house and later kept house for a relative in Fauquier County. Patty was President Lyon Tyler's secretary at William and Mary, and taught ballroom dancing to college boys. Agnes taught mandolin and guitar, while Pinkie first taught domestic science in Williamsburg schools and later kept books for Peninsula Bank and Trust Company, now part of Crestar Bank.

"Oh, Grandmother was a regular dowager," laughed Mildred Kauffmann, who basked in her aunts' attentions. Her father would drive his wife and four children by car from Newport News nearly every Sunday to visit his mother and his sisters. "Grandmother loved people and served great numbers at meals," Mrs. Kauffmann recalled. Her daughter, Kitty, took over the dining room after Mrs. Morecock's death in 1927, aided by a cook and serving girl." At Christmas and Thanksgiving, the Aunties served 30 people," Mrs. Kauffmann observed.

They favored such desserts as port wine jelly with whipped cream, trifle, charlotte russe, baked Alaska, gingerbread, coconut cake, and handturned ice cream.

As the Morecock-Rockefeller friendship grew, the philanthropist and his wife were frequent guests of the Morecocks at tea. They became "drop-in" neighbors. When the Rockefellers prepared to visit Williamsburg each April and October, they phoned the Morecocks from New York in advance to ask that they notify their housekeeper. Kitty often took delicacies to them. Once or twice "the Aunties" visited the Rockefellers in New York.

When Kitty was hospitalized in Richmond, Mr. Rockefeller called the hospital daily to ask about her. "This is John D. Rockefeller, Jr.," he told the operator on his first call. "Oh yeah?" she said. "Quit your kidding."

The Morecocks were part of Williamsburg's pre-Restoration circle that has all but disappeared. As teenagers they dated college boys, danced at hops, sang in Bruton's choir, and went out on night-time coon hunts. As women they had close friends in the garden club, church circle, Daughters of the Confederacy, King's Daughters, and Colonial Dames.

Among their friends were Mrs. Archibald McCrea of Carter's Grove, Mrs. Frank Darling of Hampton, and such Williamsburgers as Mrs. Frank Armistead, Mrs. Marston Christian, Misses Edith and Alice Smith, who owned Bassett Hall before the Rockefellers, Mr. and Mrs. George Coleman, Mrs. Herbert Lightfoot, Mrs. Kremer Hoke, Mrs. Archie Ryland, Dr. and Mrs. Lyon Tyler, Mrs. Alfred Miles, Mrs. James Southall Wilson, Mrs. Richard Mahone,

and Robert Bright. All are gone now.

"The Aunties" resisted selling their house to the Restoration until 1941. While negotiations were underway, Mr. Rockefeller remarked to Miss Kitty at tea, "Your home is charming. I'm so glad the Restoration has it." "But Mr. Rockefeller," Kitty replied, "the Restoration doesn't have it." The sale soon followed, however.

The dormer-windowed house, built in an L-shape between 1745 and 1770, was restored by the Restoration with the Morecocks' assent in 1951. It was crammed with antiques, heirlooms, mandolins, books, and pets. The Aunties kept cats and springer spaniels along with chickens and Muscovy ducks. Their rear garden looked through boxwood and trees to Bassett Hall beyond.

Friends especially remember how the Aunties loved to laugh. They relived stories like the funeral parade of the Wise Light Infantry after the Civil War. Unhappily, the parade band knew only dance tunes, so it played one as a dirge as a deceased Confederate veteran was carried to the cemetery. Everybody knew the words:

"Hop light, ladies, the cake's all dough.
Never mind the weather, so the wind don't
    blow."

When Miss Kitty, the last sister, died in May 1957, the Morecock possessions were divided among nieces and nephews. The house was taken over and rented out by Colonial Williamsburg. The Morecocks' laughter and singing died. "An era ended when the old house was dismantled," says Dr. Kimbrough. "There will never be another like the Morecocks."

40. *A Boost for the Restoration*

IN December 1929 architects for Colonial Williamsburg were beginning to restore the original form of the Wren Building at the College of William and Mary—the first project in the restoration of the eighteenth-century Virginia capital to be undertaken. They needed all the details they could learn of the first building, begun in 1695.

"Hold everything," was the word when a cablegram arrived from England. It reported the finding of a hitherto unidentified engraving in the Bodleian Library at Oxford University showing the original college building and other Williamsburg structures as they were about 1735. Immediately, architect William Graves Perry cabled the Oxford researcher, Miss Mary Goodwin, to send him a radiophoto of the engraving.

The engraving changed the architects' concept of how the college had been built. The result they achieved was the accurate reconstruction of the oldest of Williamsburg's public buildings.

Who made "the Bodleian plate," as Williamsburgers called it? When was it made, and for what unknown publication? Until recently nobody knew much about it.

Recently librarian Pearce Grove of Colonial Williamsburg went to Oxford and cleared up part of the mystery of the plate. Meantime it has been recognized as one of the most useful documents of the restoration because of its depiction not only of the three college buildings but also of Williamsburg's first Capitol and of the Governor's Palace.

Grove learned on his visit that Miss Goodwin's find (she was a cousin of the Reverend W. A. R. Goodwin) was one of 12 copper plates engraved between 1732 and 1755 for an unpublished book planned to provide maps and views of Britain's North American colonies. Grove's search has thus far turned up six of the plates in the Bodleian. The others are still sought. British and American historians have called the findings "important" and "exciting."

When the late Miss Goodwin and her friend Miss Kate Cannon went to England in 1929 to do research for Williamsburg, they pursued a lead provided by Yale University historian Charles Andrews that an engraving reposed in the Bodleian that he had identified as "Virginia. Buildings, probably in some town in Virginia or Carolina."

After she found it, Miss Goodwin persuaded

Colonial Williamsburg

Misses Mary Goodwin and Kate Cannon found the Bodleian plate in 1929 at Oxford University.

the Bodleian to make six "pulls" or impressions of the plate, two of which she immediately mailed to Williamsburg. But when architect Perry excitedly telegraphed her to rush a radio-photo and avert the two-weeks' delay then inevitable in transatlantic surface mail, Miss Goodwin later wrote, "We went to the Marconi studio at night, over in a very rough part of London. . . . When we left the office, the gentle-man in charge urged us to get to the under-ground [subway] as quickly as we could, which we did, unmolested."

The plate, which also shows native Virginia vegetation of interest to the artist, has since 1929 been widely reproduced in the lore of restored Williamsburg. In 1937 the Oxford library gave the plate to John D. Rockefeller, Jr. It is exhibited today in the Colonial Williamsburg library.

Historians once thought the Bodleian plate might have been commissioned by the Virginia scholar William Byrd II of Westover to illustrate his manuscript, *History of the Dividing Line*. (Though he wrote it in the 1730s, the publication of Byrd's account did not take place till the twentieth century.) Scholars knew the

Colonial Williamsburg

Views of pre-1732 Williamsburg buildings helped architects restore the Wren Building in 1929.

plate could not have been made till after 1732 because it depicted the President's House at the College of William and Mary, which was not built until that year.

Efforts by Pearce Grove have revealed that the engraving had been given the Bodleian Library among a collection of engraving plates, books, manuscripts, seals, medals, prints, and curiosities. They were the legacy in 1755 of the Reverend Richard Rawlinson, a Fellow of the Royal Society and an Oxford graduate who had been an English antiquary and manuscript collector. The Reverend Mr. Rawlinson was an eccentric whose will forbade the use of his collection by Scots, Irish, British colonials, members of the Royal Society, or any married person. Fortunately the conditions have not been enforced.

Says Pearce Grove, "We may never find the original drawings of those [Rawlinson] plates, or the key, but we are circulating a list of 40 questions among scholars on both sides of the Atlantic." Meanwhile, Grove keeps looking for more about that enigmatic copper plate which so greatly benefitted Williamsburg's rebuilding.

41. *Henri Mouquin's High Spirits*

IF winemaking becomes a major Virginia industry, its patron saint should be a York County man who produced fine wines during Prohibition years. He was Henri Mouquin, a once-famous New York restaurateur, who lived on a farm near Williamsburg.

Old Williamsburgers long talked about the profane, bearded eccentric who drove his two-horse carriage to town each Saturday in the 1920s and ran an open-air market next to the Powder Magazine. Locals called him "Mister Mo-kan" and said that he drank prodigious amounts of wine. Once he caught and cooked rats. He said they tasted like squirrels, but no one seems to have recorded a second opinion.

When Henri Mouquin died at the age of 94, the *New York Times* ran his obituary on page 1. It also eulogized him in an editorial, which concluded: "He was a strong character. He was a founder and a benefactor. He was a fortunate man because he knew how to live and showed the way to others."

A surviving photo shows old Henri driving his carriage over Capitol Landing Road from his farm to Williamsburg. Local resident Duncan Cocke, now retired as a Colonial Williamsburg executive, remembers Mouquin's bearded figure and his French accent. He could curse in both French and English.

To learn more about old Henri, I looked up his obituary recently in the *New York Times* of December 25, 1933. It said he had been born in Switzerland in 1837, had emigrated to the United States, had gone west to St. Louis, and then returned to New York to be a waiter at Delmonico's on lower Broadway.

In time Mouquin became famous for his own excellent restaurant. Before long he added two others, importing French wines to sell under his Mouquin label. A wine and cognac importing firm in New York still bears his name.

In its editorial, the *New York Times* said he "taught two generations the art of civilized food and drink. He provided genuine stuff at modest prices. . . . The Mouquins were the fairest of dealers. A whole school of old-time newspapermen was nurtured in his institutions. . . . In his last years he reproduced his native Switzerland in Virginia."

Mouquin's two sons carried on his New York business after he retired to York County. The old man and his lifelong Swiss wife returned to Europe at least once a year till they grew old. He made 80 transatlantic crossings in all.

In Williamsburg, Mouquin made a strong impression with his gifts of home-made wine. When he offered a glass of wine to young Merlin Larson in the 1920s, he admonished the boy to sip it slowly. "Larson boy, never gulp your liquor," Mouquin ordered. "Sip it and you'll never get drunk."

French grapes and shared his wines with visitors. He refused to own or drive a car but stuck to a two-horse carriage. He used oxen to plow his fields, as his father had done in the canton of Vaud in Switzerland.

He advocated wine in lieu of water or whiskey. "Wine eases my spirits when I am feeling

Mrs. Duncan Cocke

Henri Mouquin made wine in York County and ran an open-air Williamsburg market.

He loved to be interviewed by newspapers. "I have all I want on my estate," he said of his 1,200-acre farm, which is now part of the Camp Peary tract. "I have no doctor, no lawyer, and no preacher but plenty of leisure and time to think. New York, with Prohibition and buildings too high to see the top, no longer appeals to me." That was just before he died.

The old iconoclast especially hated Prohibition. He warmly supported New York's anti-Prohibitionist governor, Al Smith, who was defeated for the presidency by Herbert Hoover in 1928.

On his York County farm Mouquin grew

bad," he said. "A little wine and a little cognac are stimulating," he said as he merrily drank his way through Prohibition. He hated what he called progress, which he said had ruined New York. His speech was a patois of Swiss French, peppered with American idioms. One Frenchman called his profanity "superbe."

As a boy he had met Prince Louis Napoleon, who later became the emperor of France. As a young man, Henri Mouquin called on the emperor in Paris. He talked about it the rest of his life.

Despite his disdain for preachers, Mouquin's funeral was conducted by the Reverend W. A.

R. Goodwin at the Mouquin farm. Then the old individualist was laid to rest in Williamsburg's Cedar Grove Cemetery. There he lies today, he whose "name was once emblazoned in the brightest lights of Manhattan," as the *New York Times* put it in its well-merited editorial.

Fortunately, Henri Mouquin's memory is being preserved in the Williamsburg municipal building, named for Mayor Henry "Polly" Stryker. A silver cup given the Mouquins on their wedding anniversary by their son is exhibited there, together with notice of their happy Williamsburg years. It was presented by Mr. and Mrs. Duncan Cocke, to whom the old hedonist gave it before he died.

Yes, Henri Mouquin deserves to be the grand old man of Virginia wine. He preached the virtues of wine drinking long before most Americans ever tried it.

Virginia Historical Society

Farmer Henri Mouquin conducted his market near Williamsburg's Powder Magazine.

42. *Georgia O'Keeffe's Youth*

WHEN Georgia O'Keeffe died at 98 in Santa Fe in 1986, she was the second most famous woman painter in American history, excelled only by Mary Cassatt. Otherwise, they were very dissimilar painters: Miss Cassatt, a Francophile who spent most of her life with the French Impressionists, and Miss O'Keeffe, vigorously American, rooted for years in the New Mexico where she died.

But Williamsburg has a small claim to Georgia O'Keeffe, for she lived there off and on from 1903 until 1912, when her parents moved to Charlottesville. To my knowledge, she came back to Williamsburg only once after 1912. That was in 1937, when the painter was honored with a one-woman show and an honorary degree by the College of William and Mary.

Many art collectors went to her sister Anita's pueblo-style house at Abiqui, New Mexico, in later years in an effort to buy paintings for major museums, but to no avail. Georgia sold little in her declining years, and she wanted only her best works to survive.

Reading an O'Keeffe biography written in 1980 by Laurie Lisle, *Portrait of an Artist, A Biography of Georgia O'Keeffe*, I remembered the many stories of Georgia's unusual family in Williamsburg which I heard from Duncan Cocke, Leslie Cheek, and the late John Henderson. Duncan's mother, the late Christine McRae Cocke of Williamsburg, attended Chatham Hall school with Georgia when they were in their teens. She wrote this description of the Wisconsin girl, who was so different from her Virginia contemporaries:

> The most unusual thing about her was the absolute plainness of her attire. . . . Georgia's hair was drawn smoothly back from her broad, prominent forehead, and she had no bow on her head at all. . . . This strong-minded girl knew what suited her and would not be changed, though she approved of other girls dressing in frills and furbelows.

Georgia's family had been attracted to live in Williamsburg by the prospect of cheap real estate and inexpensive college educations for their seven children. For $3,500 her father bought a big white frame house on Henry Street, called Wheatlands, now torn down, and set up a grocery and creamery.

In 1908 he bought cement, made building blocks, and built an unattractive unpainted

Colonial Williamsburg

Georgia O'Keeffe's father built the family's house on Scotland Street, now torn down.

cement-block house on Scotland Street with a third-story attic, where the young O'Keeffes entertained friends on rainy days. That has been torn down, too.

Williamsburg was dirt poor in the O'Keeffes' years. The town depended on the college, then a men's school of about 200 students, plus Eastern State Hospital and the farm produce raised in James City and York counties. The O'Keeffes had no servants and didn't go to church, which made Williamsburgers think they were Catholics or atheists.

In later years Georgia O'Keeffe said of her childhood, "I was a creature of solitude. Even in a family of seven brothers and sisters, I would usually play alone, sewing dolls' clothes." But she already liked to paint. She depicted the interior of Bruton Parish church in deep purple, and she did a passable portrait of young Turner Henley, who later became a Richmond lawyer.

Georgia's mother, who was of Hungarian and Dutch ancestry, impressed Williamsburgers as aristocratic-looking, like Georgia. So also was Georgia's pretty sister Anita, four years younger than she, who later married Robert R. Young, who became head of the Chesapeake and Ohio Railway and a Palm Beach sportsman. But her Irish father, Francis O'Keeffe, seemed a rough Irish peasant.

After the O'Keeffes sold out and moved to Charlottesville in 1912, Georgia began a long period of art training under various teachers. Not until photographer Alfred Stieglitz discovered her in 1917 did she get much notice. O'Keeffe became Stieglitz's mistress, then married him in 1924 when she was 27 and he was 60.

After Stieglitz died, the solemn, individualistic Georgia moved to New Mexico, where she lived a quiet life painting the flowers and bleached desert bones she became famous for. When she returned to Williamsburg in 1937, she showed little emotion. "She seemed to be in some other world," says Leslie Cheek, who had just started William and Mary's Fine Arts Department, which got her to town. Despite the huge prices that museums came to offer for her paintings, Georgia O'Keeffe lived the last half of her life quietly, devoting herself chiefly to painting. She did most of her own housework. As she put it:

> I have no use for those who don't want to work for a living, or use their hands to do something worthwhile—to hammer a nail, plant a seed, even straighten a bed. You have to use your hands and do something with them to amount to anything, to be a creature worthy of respect. There's so much to be done, here and everywhere. Pruning, gardening, mending. Sometimes it seems I never have enough time to paint.

That was Georgia.

Chatham Hall

Teen-age Georgia O'Keeffe went from Williamsburg to Chatham Hall school.

43. *Dr. Pollard's Students*

NOBODY who knew him could easily forget whimsical, folksy John Garland Pollard, who succeeded Harry Byrd, Sr. as Virginia's chief executive from 1930 to 1934.

Pollard was the only Williamsburg resident to be governor since colonial times. He also was the first from the area to hold that office since John Gregory of James City County, who was acting governor for nine months in 1842–43.

Pollard came to William and Mary in 1922 to teach government. He largely developed the Marshall-Wythe School of Government and Citizenship, which later became the Marshall-Wythe School of Law. But Pollard loved politics even more than teaching. He had begun his career by practicing law, had been attorney general of Virginia, and had run for governor in 1917. So he went back into politics for the last 20 years of his life.

In Williamsburg, Pollard was a popular teacher and also became mayor. He organized and taught the men's bible class of Williamsburg Baptist Church. His father had been a Baptist minister, and Pollard knew the Bible and was a fine speaker. He lived with his family here in a residential area he created and called Chandler Court. Later he moved to a nearby ravine that was renamed Pollard Park.

Two big issues confronted Virginia voters in Pollard's day. One was whether Virginia should permit liquor sales and the other whether the Byrd organization should be recognized by Democrats as the voice of the party. Though a Baptist, Pollard was moderate about liquor laws. Somebody called him "the broad-minded Baptist." He was a man of tolerance and good humor. He favored Byrd because as governor Byrd had enacted Pollard's plan to reorganize Virginia's government into five streamlined departments.

One day in 1927, Governor Byrd asked Pollard to seek the Democratic nomination to succeed him when Byrd's term ended in 1930. Though Pollard was 59, he decided to run. The stock market crashed in 1929, and he knew he faced a tough four years if elected, but he wanted to be governor and to extend Byrd's reforms.

On election night, William and Mary students gathered outside Pollard's house to cheer him. When he came out, they shouted reassurance: "You're not old, Doctor Pollard." That was what he liked his friends to say whenever

Photo by Dementi from Charles Pollard

John Garland Pollard left his classroom in 1930 to become governor of Virginia.

he complained he was getting along in years.

When Pollard moved to Richmond, Virginia was in the depth of the Depression. He twice reduced state employees' paychecks by five percent, incensing many state employees but keeping the state solvent, as its constitution required.

His sense of humor never flagged. He had a Pickwickian air of amused benevolence, and he borrowed Biblical phrases and allusions from his parsonage boyhood whenever he opened his mouth. His language was simple but brightened with old sayings, dialect, and wit. He looked and talked like a preacher, even when he was dressed in cutaway and celluloid collar, as Virginia governors did before World War II.

The governor liked to quote the comment of a Jewish friend who had just heard Pollard speak in church. "This Jesus," said the friend, "He must have been quite a Jew for all you Gentiles to build so many churches to Him."

Pollard coined funny political definitions, such as: "A mugwump is a bird who sits on the fence with his mug on one side and his wump on the other." He put them all into a book he titled, *A Connotary: Definitions Not Found in Dictionaries, Collected from the Sayings of the Wise and Otherwise.* It was published by Thomas Y. Crowell in New York.

Pollard especially enjoyed his role as host for the Yorktown Sesquicentennial in October 1931, when governors of the 13 original states gathered at Yorktown for ceremonies ending with a speech by President Hoover. New York's governor then was Franklin Roosevelt, who defeated Hoover for the presidency a year later.

Despite the Depression, Pollard found the money for Virginia to start the first state art museum in America in 1934, taking advantage of a $100,000 bequest and a collection of old masters left to his native state by attorney John Barton Payne. The Virginia Museum opened in 1936 in Richmond, paid for by state and federal money plus gifts from art lovers.

Pollard finished raising money for the museum after he left office. He took no credit for it. Instead, he quoted Aunt Isabella Brockenborough, the black cook who had helped rear him and his eight brothers and sisters many years earlier in a King William County rural parsonage, not far from West Point. "You don't deserve credit for what you are," Isabella used to say. "You're just reaping the goodness of those who are dead and gone."

"Amen," said John Garland Pollard.

44. *Mysteries in Bruton Churchyard*

MENTION the name Maria Bauer to an old Williamsburg resident and you set off an explosion. For Mrs. Bauer was a California spiritualist who in 1939 persuaded the staid vestry of Bruton Parish Church to let her dig up its churchyard in search of secret codes she said were buried there. As a reporter in Newport News, I remember the incident well. Now and then I hear from fellow California spiritualists of Mrs. Bauer's.

The excavations had one good effect: they revealed the foundations of the first Bruton Parish church, a small Jacobean brick structure erected in 1683. After being studied by architects and archaeologists, the footings were covered again. They're still there, under the churchyard's tombs and grass.

Mrs. Bauer went from Williamsburg to California and wrote a book, *Foundations Unearthed*, published in 1940 by the Verulam Foundation in Glendale. It is her account of efforts to find cabalistic symbols and cult messages which she said had been left for posterity by Francis Bacon, the English philosopher-scientist who was lord chancellor to King James I.

Mrs. Bauer was one of those people who

cling to the notion that Francis Bacon actually wrote the plays attributed to Shakespeare. More than that, she believed Bacon anticipated the American nation with supernatural accuracy in his 1627 tract, *The New Atlantis*, wherein he described a utopian society based on science. Somehow Mrs. Bauer got the idea that some of Bacon's secret lore—encoded in anagrams and mixed up with Masonic symbols—had been brought to Virginia in the seventeenth century by Nathaniel Bacon, Sr., who is buried in Bruton churchyard. In *Foundations Unearthed*, she wrote:

> Shortly before the Bacon Rebellion (in 1676) and in connection with the planned removal of the Virginia Capital to Williamsburg [from Jamestown], the records were brought to their final resting place in a great vault beneath the tower center of the first brick church in Bruton Parish.

Mrs. Bauer got along well at first. She persuaded the Restoration to excavate around the Bruton Church steeple, where the foundations of the first Bruton church were then thought to lie. When the excavations uncovered none, she examined a Williamsburg map drawn by

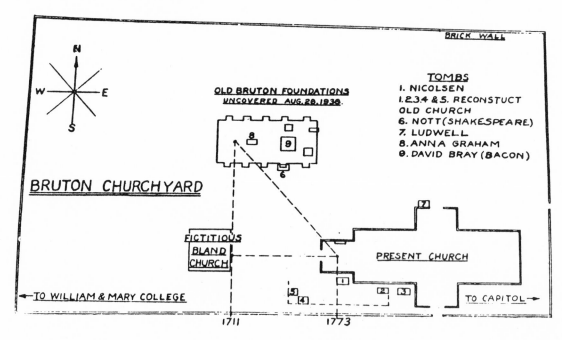

Author's collection

Spiritualist Maria Bauer drew a map of Bruton churchyard and wrote of her findings.

Theodorick Bland in 1699. From it she correctly deduced that the first Bruton church actually lay 60 feet to the north of the present 1715 church.

The Rockefeller organization refused to bear the costs of any further digging, so Mrs. Bauer persuaded Mayor Channing Hall and Bruton's senior warden, Wynne Roberts, to appropriate vestry funds for the purpose.

Sure enough, when the site recommended by Mrs. Bauer was dug up in August 1938, it revealed the foundations of the 1683 church. They were about 66 feet long and 29 feet wide, and had brick buttresses to support the outer walls, like St. Luke's Church, built about the same time near Smithfield and still standing.

Because the first Bruton Church had been poorly built and proved too small for Williamsburg after the town became Virginia's capital in 1699, the present and larger Bruton was built to replace it. The 1683 church was then torn down and covered with cemetery burials.

Three days after the foundations were revealed, Mrs. Bauer wrote, the vestry had them covered up again. She was angry, for she was still searching them for a Bacon vault. "The vestry suggested that the search for the vault be delayed until the excitement died down," she writes. She was further offended when the press reported that the vestry had found the first Bruton foundations, without crediting her. She felt cheated, she wrote.

Finally Mrs. Bauer got permission from the vestry to dig for the casket of one Anna Graham within the old church foundation area, for she believed the Graham casket held Bacon's secrets. But she was disappointed again "when we were not allowed to investigate the casket or the lettering on it in brass tacks."

Because Bacon had been a Mason, she got in touch with Masonic leaders to ask their support, but they were unable to help her.

Now thoroughly miffed with most of the people she had dealt with in Williamsburg, Mrs.

Bauer returned to California and wrote her book. In it she expressed confidence that someday the Graham casket would be dug up and Francis Bacon's legacy to the New World would provide "medicinal aid toward soothing the birth pains of a new age."

From her home in California, Mrs. Bauer later indicated her continued interest in the secret signs she feels Francis Bacon left behind him. She hoped others will take up the project.

It all gave Williamsburg a lot to talk about in 1938.

Colonial Williamsburg

Workmen dug up foundations of the first Bruton church in 1938 in a quest for buried relics.

St. George Tucker, Revolutionary soldier, established a dynasty in Williamsburg.

Colonial Williamsburg

45. *Tuckers, Colemans, and History*

OF all the families who've lived in Williamsburg these 350 years, the Tuckers probably have been the most prominent. The house that St. George Tucker started when he moved here in 1788 has been occupied ever since by his descendants. In fact, his great-great-granddaughter, Dr. Janet Kimbrough, still lives in the Tucker-Coleman House.

The Tuckers are long-lived peopled. They're also traditionalists, sticking to the law, medicine, and divinity as professions. Until the last two generations, most Tucker males went into one of those fields or became a law teacher or dean.

A notable exception was George Preston Coleman, the father of Janet Kimbrough, who lived in the Tucker-Coleman house until he died in 1951. He was a civil engineer and a pioneer in highway building. The Coleman Bridge at Yorktown is named for him. He was the son of Cynthia Beverley Tucker, who helped found the Association for Preservation of Virginia Antiquities and who married Dr. Charles Coleman, a nineteenth-century Williamsburg doctor. George Coleman's grandfather was Nathaniel Beverley Tucker, son of St. George, who taught

law at William and Mary before the Civil War.

George Coleman married a Lynchburg woman, Mary Haldane Begg, who helped start Williamsburg's library and other civic organizations. I remember "May" Coleman in Williamsburg in the 1950s. She was a thin, bespectacled lady who was helpful to researchers because she'd been in the thick of Williamsburg since she came here as George Coleman's fiancée in 1899 and stayed until she died in 1967. She and Miss Annie Chapman had started the library (now Williamsburg Regional Library) in her house, and her husband had been mayor and president of the Peninsula Bank, now part of Crestar Bank. She was a friend of Abby and John D. Rockefeller, Jr.

May Coleman spoke such an odd Scottish-Virginian argot that Winston Churchill couldn't understand her when they sat side by side at a Williamsburg dinner in 1946. Turning to his host, Churchill whispered, "What lengwidge is this leddy speaking?"

Handsome George Coleman proposed to May Begg in 1897, but they had to wait for marriage until he earned more money. He brought her to Williamsburg in 1899 to meet his mother, Cynthia Tucker Coleman. May wrote then that she found the village modernizing.

"I arrived just as the change was coming," she wrote. "The railroad, the celebration of the Centennial at Yorktown, with the resulting tourists, and the growth of the College all brought about the beginnings of the new era."

May Coleman kept a diary, wrote charming letters, and published two books, *Virginia Silhouettes* in 1934 and *St. George Tucker, Citizen of No Mean City* in 1938. She also contributed poems and sketches to *A Williamsburg Scrapbook* published by the Williamsburg Garden Club in 1932.

Researchers frequently consult May Coleman's 1906-1967 diaries. (Her daughter, Janet Kimbrough, stipulates that they not publish any of her mother's personal comments.) They're full of useful data on local events as well as family matters. She was encouraged in her record-keeping by Harold Shurtleff, the first Colonial Williamsburg historian, who came to town in the 1930s. As a result, her diaries are a good account of the Rockefeller Restoration from 1928 until her death.

May Coleman didn't like everything about the Restoration. Once she wrote: "Intimate as we are with our surroundings, and each one of us brought up with firm convictions of the authenticity of the legends connected with different houses, it has been very irritating to have them exploded or ignored by strangers primed with information gained by 'research.'"

The Colemans had two daughters: Janet, who became a doctor, married and divorced Dr. Raymond Kimbrough, and then came back to the Tucker house as its last life tenant. After her death it will become the property of Colonial Williamsburg. Her sister, Cynthia, married Restoration architect Singleton Moorehead. Both are dead.

George Preston Coleman became one of the first Virginia highway commissioners but fell out with Harry Byrd's pay-as-you-go highway policies, resigned and came home in 1927 to be a banker and mayor. He died in 1951. His wife lived on in the Tucker house with her sister, Mrs. Isobel Hubbard. They were bright and independent ladies.

Though the Tuckers and Colemans were progressive in most ways, Mrs. Coleman was sympathetic with a few elderly Williamsburg residents who preferred to see their town poor and shabby rather than restored and commercial. She wrote: "It seems curious that the very movement which is intended to preserve the beauty and dignity of Williamsburg's past should be the means of opening the floodgates through which will be swept away the last vestiges of the old, simple life."

Nobody in Williamsburg was better able to record the transition of Williamsburg from a nineteenth-century ruin than the little lady who viewed the world from the book-lined rooms of St. George Tucker's old house. The Tuckers and Colemans made Williamsburg history.

The Tucker-Coleman House on Courthouse Green has been the seat of a prolific family.

Colonial Williamsburg

An automobile tunnel for the Colonial Parkway was dug beneath Duke of Gloucester Street in the 1930s.

IV.
Williamsburg
in a Global Age

1946 – 1989

46. *When Ike and Winnie Came to Town*

WHEN General Dwight Eisenhower learned on a European battlefield in 1945 that President Roosevelt had died, he exclaimed, "Jesus Christ, who is the vice president?"

That's what Ike confided to his hosts when he came to Williamsburg with Winston Churchill on March 8, 1946, after defeating the Axis in Europe. The two men were wildly applauded when Winnie addressed the General Assembly in Richmond and then he and Ike boarded a train for Williamsburg as guests of the Rockefellers.

To those who were there, "Ike and Winnie Day" is a cherished memory. Intimate glimpses of that day have been revealed by two of their 1946 Williamsburg hosts, Mr. and Mrs. Kenneth Chorley. He was president of Colonial Williamsburg from 1935 to 1958. His widow, the former stage and nightclub singer Jean Travers, lives quietly near Princeton, New Jersey. Her memoirs, *From Harlem to Buckingham Palace*, have been privately printed for friends and family.

Churchill seemed to the Chorleys a demanding guest. He pressured Kenneth into playing gin rummy en route to Williamsburg and drank endless scotches. "He is an extraordinary person and has great vitality," Chorley wrote, "but he is a snob, and a snob of the first order. I should imagine he is a difficult person to live with." Churchill had just stepped down as Britain's prime minister, after his Conservatives lost to Labor.

The gin game began soon after the VIP private train left Richmond, bearing Ike, Winnie, Governor Colgate Darden, Mr. and Mrs. John D. Rockefeller 3rd, the Chorleys and many aides. An Eisenhower staffer summoned Chorley to Churchill's car.

"Do you play gin rummy?" Churchill asked Chorley.

"Yes, I do," Chorley replied.

"Well, why don't we have a game?" Churchill asked.

When the ex-P. M. proposed they play for ten cents a point, "I nearly dropped dead," Chorley recalled. "I think the most I had ever played for was a half cent or a cent a point. . . . But having said what I did, there wasn't anything I could do but say 'Fine.'"

Chorley won $35 right off, but the second game was cut short when the train reached Williamsburg and Mayor Channing Hall came

Colonial Williamsburg

*After carriage horses bolted, Williamsburg officials got
Churchill and Eisenhower out for a walking tour.*

aboard to greet the visitors. Dismayed at the interruption, Churchill proposed that Chorley travel with him to Washington that night to play gin. Chorley couldn't, but the two returned to Churchill's rail car before midnight to finish a second game. While it dragged on, Chorley remembered that Governor Darden was waiting to say goodbye. "Well," Churchill replied, "I guess he will wait until I'm finished, won't he?"

John D. Rockefeller 3rd kibitzed briefly and told Chorley, "If you need any help just let me know." At that, Churchill quipped, "When you play gin rummy with me, you need the backing of the Rockefellers." This time Chorley lost $37.50. Deducting his earlier winnings, he handed the pleased Churchill $2.50. "I was up against an expert," Chorley lamented to Eisenhower.

During the games Churchill "continually ordered scotches, but he showed no ill effects of it whatsoever," Chorley noted. To keep up with the Britisher, Chorley drank a half-dozen highballs in short order. Meanwhile, Churchill smoked a cigar and muttered to himself. Once he growled, "America, the greatest country in

Colonial Williamsburg

Williamsburg's President Chorley led Churchill and Eisenhower on their 1946 victory visit.

the world. God look after it!" Churchill discarded a king from his hand with the snort, "Who wants any quarter with royalty?" When he picked up another king, he muttered, "Well, somebody has to look after them."

Chorley noted a contrast in the two leaders' response to the crowds. "Ike got off the train perfectly naturally and informally and waved to the crowd," Chorley wrote. "Not Mr. Churchill. When he came to the platform . . . and the people started to clap, he stopped. He waved, took off his hat, and just milked it for all it was worth." Williamsburg streets were crowded with onlookers.

Disaster threatened when Ike and Winnie boarded an eighteenth-century carriage to be

driven through Williamsburg. Wrote Chorley, "the horses were frightened by flashlight bulbs and backed right into a circle of grass in front of the [Governor's] Palace. . . . I was frightened to death, but Churchill and Eisenhower did not seem concerned. We got them out."

At an evening reception at the Williamsburg Inn, Churchill told Chorley he didn't want cocktails but wanted scotch with dinner. "Oh, yes, and we're going to have champagne," Chorley assured him. To that Churchill replied, "Oh, that's wonderful. I'll have both!"

In her memoirs, Jean Chorley recalls that Clementine Churchill said on arrival, "I don't plan to wear a hat today." She quickly added, "Oh, please, everyone do exactly as she wishes.

I don't like to wear a hat and am going to wear what you Americans call a snood." Daughter Sarah Churchill piped up, "And I'm going to wear this hat (indicating one she wore) because it's new. I bought it in Washington for $2.98."

Jean Chorley sat next to Eisenhower at dinner that night. He talked about cooking and described his beef stew. When she mentioned President Roosevelt's death, Ike described his receipt of radio news of the death while visiting General George Patton's Allied headquarters in Europe at midnight, in company with General Omar Bradley. As Jean Chorley remembers it,

Ike said, "General Patton . . . always shaved the last thing at night, and he would turn on the radio for the 12 o'clock [midnight] news. A little while later . . . General Patton dashed into the room with lather on one side of his face and said, "The president is dead and they're swearing in the vice president!" Eisenhower responded, "Jesus Christ, who is the vice president?"

When Eisenhower later sent the Chorleys his autographed book, *Crusade in Europe*, they noted he repeated the story in the book, except for the remark about the vice president.

Jean Chorley was surprised that Ike said of

Colonial Williamsburg

Churchill and Eisenhower were hosted by John D. Rockefeller 3rd, at center in limousine.

his postwar job as chief of staff under Truman, "I don't like it at all. Too much red tape. When I was out in the field I made decisions and gave orders . . . whereas in Washington I make decisions and give orders and they get all hung up in red tape." When Mrs. Chorley blamed Ike's situation on "the democratic process," Ike objected. "I consider the democratic process to be when you have confidence in a man you let him go ahead and do what he thinks ought to be done instead of getting in his way."

Unpersuaded, Jean Chorley told Ike, "Well,

General, even the president . . . can't just go ahead and do what he wants." Ike replied, "No, he can't, and that is why when Mr. Truman said to me, 'Ike, get yourself ready for 1948,' I said to him, 'Mister President, if you have no intention of running in 1948, I can tell you now I don't want any part of 1948 or any other time."

As it turned out, Truman did choose to run in 1948 and was reelected president. But Eisenhower made it four years later, to Jean Chorley's satisfaction.

In the Raleigh Tavern, Ike, Governor Darden, Field Marshal Wilson, and Churchill brandished clay pipes.

Colonial Williamsburg

47. *Dr. Swem and His Discoveries*

I think of them as witnesses of the creation—those dwindling survivors of the enthusiasts who revived eighteenth-century Williamsburg and the College of William and Mary during the 1920s and 1930s. They converted a sleepy college and a decrepit town into the exciting center that Williamsburg is today. There aren't many of them left.

They were a diverse and unusual group. Some were natives of Williamsburg, but most were specialists brought in after John D. Rockefeller, Jr. gave the go ahead to Dr. W. A. R. Goodwin to buy and restore a few key colonial buildings, later expanded to the whole town.

At the same time, President Julian A. C. Chandler was expanding William and Mary, which he took over in 1919 as a just-turned-coed college of a few hundred students. The college and Colonial Williamsburg grew big together, scrapping at first, but now at peace.

One of the key figures in those years was Earl Gregg Swem, William and Mary's librarian and a seminal figure in Virginia archival history. He gathered manuscripts of Williamsburg's past, and he made William and Mary one of the best sources of colonial records in the United States.

"Archives" is a dull word to most people, but collecting those manuscript letters of Revolutionary greats was a heated and exciting contest in Earl Swem's lifetime. Ivy League libraries, the Library of Congress, and the Huntington Library in California had made the scholarly world conscious of the need to save America's early records. Vast numbers of such papers in the 1920s slumbered in Virginia attics and trunks, many being bought by manuscript dealers and well-financed out-of-state institutions. Many were removed that should have stayed in Virginia.

Earl Swem was brought by President Chandler to William and Mary in 1920 to help the college get its share of those vital early documents. He was a small, delicate-looking man with a thin voice and a tendency to petulance, but his life was dedicated after 1920 to reviving William and Mary and building it as a center of colonial study. He and Chandler revived the *William and Mary Historical Quarterly*, and he went to bat successfully against big-money libraries to beg and buy historical manuscripts.

Duke and the University of North Carolina were very active then in archive-building, along with the University of Virginia and fast-rising Stanford and Texas Universities. Tiny Earl

William and Mary

Earl Gregg Swem and William Harkins, his librarian sucessor, examine a manuscript.

Swem worked closely with Chandler and William and Mary's fund raiser, Dr. W. A. R. Goodwin, to try to talk Virginia manuscript owners into giving or selling theirs to the college. After all, they argued, the logical place for Virginia records was in Virginia.

Dr. Swem increased William and Mary's library from 30,000 books to 450,000 by the time he retired in 1940. He liked to tell of the Tennessee woman who reciprocated his help in finding her ancestors' graves in Surry County by giving the college 145 letters Jefferson had written to her collateral ancestor, William Short, an alumnus of William and Mary. They help give the college one of the best Jefferson manuscript collections in existence.

I wrote an article in the *Richmond Times-Dispatch* in the 1940s applauding Dr. Swem's gallant uphill battle to retain Virginia's archives against big bucks "outside" libraries, and he became my friend for life. After I moved to

Williamsburg, I saw a lot of him until he and Mrs. Swem left their book-filled house in Chandler Court in the 1950s to retire to Louisville, where they died.

Swem, born in the midwest, grew up with a passionate enthusiasm for Virginia's colonial years and in the 1940s compiled his monumental "Swem Index" of Virginia history, one of the primary resources for colonial historians. William and Mary named its library in the 1950s for him. Its size has been doubled since then.

Though Swem looked like a frail Mister Chips, he was a tough little man. He never forgave Dr. Goodwin for not ensuring that Williamsburg's Restoration remained under the college's control, as was first conceived. And he refused for years to let Colonial Williamsburg photograph the Frenchman's Map in the college library to help restore Williamsburg after 1926. Only the intervention of John Bentley of Hampton, then a recent William and Mary graduate, enabled Colonial Williamsburg researchers to get a hand-drawn copy. It has been called the Bible of Williamsburg restorationists.

All that is long past. Today the ranks of those who were present at the creation in the Goodwin-Rockefeller-Chandler-Swem years are thinning fast. But what an exciting community they've left us.

Colonial Williamsburg

Visitors trace tomb inscriptions in Bruton Churchyard, a genealogist's delight.

48. *Merchants Square Makes History*

ONE of the success stories of Williamsburg is Merchants Square, a two-block area at the west end of Duke of Gloucester Street, adjoining the College of William and Mary. Since the 1930s it has become one of the most popular specialty shopping areas in the east, ranking with Boston's Faneuil Hall area and Baltimore's Harbor Place.

My hat's off to Colonial Williamsburg for its imagination. It has made a once-nondescript city block into a refreshing collection of boutiques, restaurants, ice cream parlors, and sidewalk benches for girl-watchers and other dreamers.

Each summer Merchants Square is alive with families in T-shirts, shorts, and Adidas shoes, slurping ice cream and marveling at what God and Rockefeller have wrought. Even in winter, sunny days bring out dozens of sleek young William and Mary joggers who race from the college down Duke of Gloucester Street while sidewalk idlers and shoppers look on.

I'm not sure how John D. Rockefeller, Jr. would view all this. As an Edwardian gentleman who never appeared without suit and tie, he'd probably be taken aback by all those bare arms, legs, navels, and chests. But then again,

even John D. was always aware of the old bottom line. Merchants Square is a shopper's paradise, and its landlord is happy. Rockefeller started restoring Williamsburg so that "the Future may learn from the Past." But on Merchants Square a lot of Pasts are learning from the Futures. It has livened up the old greatly and provided needed space for shops and artisans catering to collectors and the public.

Williamsburg has found the traveler loves to bring home high-style clothes, food, and gifts from the attractive and imaginative shops. The two-block area Williamsburg has created is so successful that it is being expanded to nearby Prince George and Francis Streets.

I remember the Square when I came to live in Williamsburg in 1951. It was then called "the Business Block," for it housed the town's main stores and restaurants. It had an A&P (it did the greatest business per square foot of any A&P in the nation), the town's only bank, its only hardware store, its only department store, a women's wear shop, a men's shop, and restaurants known as "The Corner Greek's" and "The Middle Greek's."

Those restaurants were favorite hangouts of William and Mary students, especially after

Colonial Williamsburg

"College Corner" in the 1920s was a mixture of homes and smalltown businesses.

beer was legalized. The specialties were delicatessen sandwiches named for Jefferson, Madison, and other WASPs, who never themselves knew the glories of knockwurst, pastrami, feta cheese, or bologna.

In dormer-windowed offices above the stores were the town's barbers, lawyers, beauty parlors, dentists, and collection agencies. It was a soft-sell town.

Then Colonial Williamsburg began to realize what a gold mine it had in that shopping block —if only they could move the non-tourist local stores off Duke of Gloucester and replace them with travel-related tourist shops. As a result, the Foundation in the 1950s built the town's first shopping center on Williamsburg's Richmond Road. It has become the town's major shopping area, with its own banks, supermarkets, and chain stores.

That freed Duke of Gloucester to become a tourist paradise—a handsome city block with its own built-in parking areas, containing tasteful specialty shops, imaginatively displaying gifts, souvenirs, crafts, luxury items, and other impulse goods for the nearly two million visitors who surge through Merchants Square each year.

Ghiradelli Square in San Francisco was the inspiration for Merchants Square. If you've been there, you know it's an abandoned chocolate factory that's been converted into a bazaar of boutiques and seductions for upper-income travelers. Since then, other tourist towns have built similar shop-and-browse-and-eat areas. You'll find them at Hilton Head, Savannah, Charleston, and many other places.

The revamped Merchants Square increased its appeal by adding two good restaurants. One

Colonial Williamsburg

At "College Corner" stood students' hangout with restaurant and bus station.

was the Trellis, a high-style gourmet eatery launched by three local businessmen. The other was A Good Place to Eat, opened by Colonial Williamsburg. Other good restaurants followed. The eateries hold visitors twice as long in Merchants Square as the visitor used to spend. They're especially popular at lunch, for the Square is next to Duke of Gloucester's exhibit buildings. Colonial Williamsburg tour buses, which circuit the town at frequent intervals, drop off hundreds of travelers at the Square each lunchtime, where they wine, dine, and spend money.

Merchants Square's construction in the 1930s was authorized by John D. Rockefeller, Jr. originally to allay fears of Duke of Gloucester shopkeepers that the Restoration would leave no room in town for their businesses.

Accordingly, Rockefeller planners built the colonial-style business block at the college end of Duke of Gloucester Street, though no precise precedent for it existed.

Some people in those days thought the restoration had made a mistake to build structures which visitors would take to be original eigtheenth-century shops. Abby Aldrich Rockefeller, the philanthropist's wife, said it was the only major mistake she thought had been made in Williamsburg's transformation.

Mistake or not, however, Merchants Square is today Williamsburg's lively town square, full of Americans learning a little history and having a good time.

Colonial Williamsburg

The closing of Duke of Gloucester Street permitted growth of Merchants Square near the college.

49. *Jimmy, the Pottery Man*

WORLD War II was over. At the Williamsburg Pottery in Lightfoot, customers were poking through dusty bowls and glasses, picking and choosing bargains. Suddenly a whistle sounded. Instantly, a dozen stock boys—black and white teenagers—dropped their work to rush outside to the basketball court and line up for the morning game.

The man who blew the whistle and led the game was James Maloney, who ten years earlier had paid $150 for that half-acre on Route 60 and launched what is now James City County's biggest locally-owned business. Now over 70, but lean and active, Jimmy Maloney takes in more than $50 million yearly at his city of warehouses. What started as a saltglaze pottery some 50 years ago now sells just about everything.

The kiln Maloney built in 1938 is now a 112-acre complex of shops selling clothes, plants, souvenirs, and household goods. It's a shopper's paradise—and often a traffic nightmare.

Maloney's rule is to sell at rock-bottom. Like Henry Ford, he believes low markups bring sales. His parking lot proves he's right. Seven days a week, the Pottery draws an average of over 5,000 shoppers a day.

Tall, bespectacled Jimmy is unimpressed. Old and young, including his employees, call him "Jimmy." He's given up basketball, but he's become a racquetball and tennis nut. And he and his wife, the former Gloria Thacker of Charlottesville, work as hard as ever unless they're on a buying trip to Mexico, Taiwan, Japan, or some other pottery supplier. Working with them are their son, Fred, three daughters, and a nephew. A son-in-law and a daughter-in-law are also officers. "Everybody works around this place," beams Jimmy.

Maloney was born in Newport News in 1912, the grandson of an Irish Catholic immigrant to America in 1868. Jimmy's father, a brass fitter at the shipyard, had five children. Jimmy—the third—went to St. Vincent's Catholic School and graduated from Newport News High. In the Depression, the only job he could find was on Tom Brabrand's dairy farm on the James River near Jamestown, later bought by Elder Michaux's Gospel-Spreading Association. "Life now is nothing like life then," Jimmy says. "The Depression taught me good lessons."

In James City the gangling ex-high school basketball player met Paul Griesenauer, whose Jamestown Colony Pottery at Pinedell was turning out eigtheenth-century ware. Griesenauer hired Jimmy to load and unload his kiln. He also taught him to be a potter. "It was hard," Maloney recalls. "I still have bumps on my head from hitting the kiln roof when I stood up."

After three years Maloney decided to open his own pottery near Michie Tavern on Monticello Mountain near Charlottesville. There he met his future wife, a slim girl who was walking up the mountain to pick apples. The marriage is happy. "She's the greatest helper in the world," he says.

After five years at Charlottesville, Maloney was attracted to Lightfoot by the sudden growth of Williamsburg tourism. He was also given a contract by the Restoration to make reproductions of eigtheenth-century saltglaze ware for Colonial Williamsburg. Other craftsmen like Max Rieg, Don Works, and Palin Thorley also made items for CW's "licensed reproductions" program. Maloney still makes saltglaze for the Restoration.

Jimmy made big roadside signs to advertise his kiln, offering cheap "seconds." More and more travelers stopped to buy, and he and Gloria trucked other of their wares to vendors in nearby states. "We nearly starved to death, but we persisted," he says. "We wagoned all over. Sometimes we'd come back with an empty truck, sometimes half empty. We had little retail trade at first at Lightfoot."

The Maloneys did their own hard work. Jimmy dug a well to provide kiln water, built his kiln, and created a rough-hewn workshop and residence. He and Gloria wrapped customer purchases in newspaper (their clerks still do). They had no cash register but added up figures on a blackboard. They put the day's receipts in a purse and counted it at night on their bed.

When World War II interrupted tourism, Jimmy tried to enlist. He was turned down for poor eyesight, but worked through the war at the Yorktown Naval Weapons Station.

After the war, Jimmy enlarged his plant and moved his family to a second floor room he built over the kiln. After his father retired from the shipyard, Jimmy built on a room for "Pops" and "Nanny." Jimmy's older brother, Andy, and Gloria's sister and brother-in-law, Mr. and Mrs. John Venable, also joined the force.

Author's collection

Jimmy Mahoney's pottery grew into a huge crafts market and Lightfoot tourist magnet.

New wares were added after the war, swelling the Pottery to its present size. Jimmy began buying overruns from eastern glass and china factories, and hauling them to Lightfoot on his truck. They contained a little of everything: some fine, some imperfect, and some "dogs" that had to be half-priced to sell on the Pottery's "Skid Row." Many American households now contain Maloney merchandise.

From its start, the Pottery used makeshift buildings. Shoppers say they add to the bargain atmosphere. The first shops had dirt floors, but Jimmy's insurers made him add cement. Dogs and chickens once wandered in at will, but shoppers liked the confusion. "It's a treasure hunt," one shopper said. "You don't know what you'll find. That's exciting."

The four Maloney children worked right along with their parents. They still do. Fred, the eldest, began traveling with his father in his teens. He bought carloads of bargains and drove them to Lightfoot. Now he's president of the family corporation, which Jimmy chairmans. Gloria is second in line.

The Pottery introduced Williamsburg to discount malls and "second" shops, changing the character of Lightfoot and Toano. Route 60, once farmland, became prime property. Realtors say the Pottery helped change Richmond Road into "Bicentennial Boulevard"—a string of motels, restaurants, and tourist shops. "It's the hottest real estate in the Williamsburg area," says one realtor. He credits Jimmy Maloney.

Tour buses now include stops at the Pottery. One recent day brought 168 at one time. In York, Pennsylvania, the Red Coach line offers a weekly "Historic Williamsburg" trip which spends more time at the Pottery than in the Historic Area.

Writer Tina Jeffrey once persuaded publicity-shy Jimmy Maloney to talk about himself. Some typical Maloney views, as quoted in Mrs. Jeffrey's booklet, "The Bizarre Bazaar":

> Customers don't come because they like us. They don't come because we're great craftsmen. They come to save money.
>
> The bottom line is cash-flow. It's the only thing that counts.
>
> I've never had an office in my life. I don't believe in offices.
>
> We are not very socially oriented. . . . Life is too short to be a joiner.
>
> They (my stock boys) are all named "Hoss." That's what I call 'em. It's easier.

Jimmy Maloney is a Depression-era success story: a motivated man who used his talent and opportunity to achieve for his children what he himself missed as a boy. He's a self-made multi-millionaire who took advantage of the Williamsburg tourist boom created by the Restoration.

50. *Williamsburg's Good Ol' Boys*

THE revival of Williamsburg and its college after the 1920s made the town an exciting mixture of native and newcomer, Southerner and Yankee. New professors and Rockefeller executives discovered coon-hunting and bootleg whiskey.

The "good old boys" invited the new arrivals to hunt and fish. Poker clubs took in new members. A Rotary Club was formed to meld town and gown, "come-here" and "stay-put."

A lot of newcomers got acquainted with the *Irene and Pearl*, a York River motorboat that carried eight or ten men on week-end fishing trips for several decades until the 1960s. She was just an old oyster boat, but the *Irene and Pearl* spread mayhem whenever she sailed from the Queen's Creek Marina on a two-day poker and fishing party. The fishing was really a cover-up to appease unhappy wives. Only one of all the guests who put out to sea on her ever brought along a fishing pole. The rest had better things to do.

Pittman Roane, who was co-owner and host aboard the *Irene and Pearl*, started inviting a few friends on his trips in the years after World War II. Williamsburg in those days had several colorful poker and hunting groups which had

survived from the pre-World War I era, before the Restoration began to change the town. "Pitt picked fellows he knew would get along and wouldn't mind getting seasick," recalls Robert Walker, Williamsburg's recent mayor, and one of the survivors of the voyages.

Co-host occasionally with the easygoing Roane was big Bob Wallace, a one-time William and Mary football star who was co-owner with Roane of the York River Oyster Company at Capahosic in Gloucester County. Roane used the boat during the winter to dredge oysters. In summer, he took friends cruising.

The wit in the group was John Warburton, whose insults of his fellow voyagers kept the crowd laughing. Another antic guest was Yelverton Kent, another William and Mary ex-athlete of early days. Other *Irene and Pearl* faithfuls, all dead, were Dick Mahone, Sr., Dick Benschoten, John Lewis, Jr., Piggy Hogge, Owen Latham, and Bob Duncan.

Besides Bob Walker, the only other passengers still around are Edwin Kendrew, ex-vice president of Colonial Williamsburg; I. L. "Rod" Jones, ex-treasurer; Lenny Graves, a retired merchant; and Roosevelt Harris, steward and cook of the voyages.

183

Colonial Williamsburg

The Pulaski Club met in the back room of Henry Cole's shop
on Duke of Gloucester Street across from Bruton Church.

The *Irene and Pearl* wasn't much to look at, but she was seaworthy. Most of her 50-foot-long hull was left uncovered to hold oysters dredged up by her crew. A small cabin at her stern contained the pilot's wheel, engine, two bunks, and a galley for cooking. "Most of the passengers slept on hammocks, pallets, or mattresses on deck," Bob Walker recalls. "It was awful when it rained."

Robert Duncan, who served for years as president of Williamsburg's United Virginia Bank, preferred sleeping in a hammock, as he had done as a youth in the Navy. Other prankish guests once tied him into it as he slept.

Survivors Walker and Jones like to recall the time Yel Kent jumped in Chesapeake Bay to rescue a stack of dollar bills blown overboard while he played poker with John Warburton. Climbing back on deck exhausted, Kent handed the wet bills to Warburton, who counted them and then loudly demanded, "Damn you, Kent, where's the other dollar?"

Colonial Williamsburg

Corner Billiards adjoined Bob Wallace's College Shop at "College Corner" in the 1930s.

When Pitt Roane's summer cruise guests grew older, he tried inviting a doctor along for medical emergencies. However, the doctor was tipsy before the *Irene and Pearl* had even traversed Queen's Creek on her way to the York River. He is immortalized in his fellow passengers' memory as "The Creek Doctor."

Another shipmate once was put ashore at a Chesapeake Bay port to telephone Williamsburg and have his wife inform other passengers' wives when the *Irene and Pearl* would return. "Who are the other passengers?" the wife asked. "Damned if I remember," he replied boozily.

Only once in its voyages did the *Irene and Pearl* suffer a major accident. While sailing up the York just before suppertime one night, the vessel began to leak badly. Water reached up around the ankles of Roosevelt Harris, who was cooking in the galley. "Go on with supper, Roosevelt," shouted Pitt Roane as he calmly steered the *Irene and Pearl* onto a mud flat while the meal could be served and the leak repaired.

Like most of the old oyster boat's passengers, the *Irene and Pearl* finally reached her end. When Walker last heard of her, her tiny rear cabin was barely visible in shoal waters near Capahosic Creek on the shore of the York River near Clay Bank. "But we had our share of good times while she lasted," Walker recalls happily. "I'd love to take another trip with all those guys."

Most of the *Irene and Pearl* crowd were also members of Rotary, the first civic club to invade Williamsburg in the 1920s. Unlike other Rotarians, Williamsburg Rotarians proved to be an unorthodox group who didn't take themselves or their rituals very seriously. They came to the Thursday night meetings in high humor, prepared to bait the president with every known devilment. If they knew the night's speaker, they'd heckle him mercilessly. One member lit a firecracker behind the speaker's podium one night.

It was meant to be good-humored, but you could see it shocked visiting Rotarians from more orthodox clubs. I could appreciate their surprise as Yel Kent, Lockert Bemiss, or Tom Savage filibustered the presiding officer in the midst of the meeting. "Do you behave like this all the time?" visitors would ask.

In a way, though, the club served as a useful mediator among the small empires that make up the pumpkin pie called Williamsburg. It brought together a few individualists who antedated the Restoration—oldtimers like Mayor H.M. "Polly" Stryker and Postmaster Merritt Foster—with professors like Dick Morton and Restoration heads like Ed Kendrew, Rod Jones, and Charlie Hackett.

Williamsburg Rotary in those days was full of small town poker foursomes that played for an hour or two each Thursday after Rotary adjourned. Some foursomes had survived for years—the then-traditional weekly night out when men relaxed over cards, bourbon, smoke, and gossip. Rotary also provided a cover- up for henpecked husbands whose wives objected to gambling, even for penny-ante stakes.

Some wives never did learn that those long Rotary evenings their husbands complained of were actually one-hour Rotary dinner meetings followed by two or three hours with the cards. Once in a while some wife would ask, "What in the world do you Rotarians find to talk about for four hours?" I never did say.

It's surprising how little it took to amuse small town Williamsburg. The members of the Senior Club, the Junior Club, and the Seven-

Thomas A. Williams

Dr. Henry M. "Polly" Stryker was Williamsburg's popular mayor from 1948 to 1968.

Ups gloried in belonging to poker clubs that reached back to Prohibition and beyond. They overlapped a little with the hunting clubs in pre-Rockefeller Williamsburg. Some hunt clubs even had clubhouses in Williamsburg's outskirts. Once yearly they'd band together and put on a wild game dinner, with stewards like Roosevelt Harris and Fred Epps, Sr. serving up rabbit, squirrel, venison, muskrat, and raccoon.

All that was good for Williamsburg. Rotary was a catalyst for a lot of divergent people and ideas back in the old days, and I guess it still is.

51. *The Greening of the College*

THE grounds of William and Mary form an arboretum of unusual trees and landscaping that is added to every year. The College's arboreal record began in 1694, when Sir John Evelyn wrote in England that a gardener had been sent to Virginia "on purpose to make and plant the garden designed for the new College."

The earliest known print of the Williamsburg buildings, engraved about 1735, shows formal topiary plantings and fences linking the Wren Building and its newly built flanking structures, the Brafferton and the President's House.

An advertisement by the college gardener, Thomas Crease, in Williamsburg's *Virginia Gazette* in 1738 offered to sell flower roots, seed, and trees, presumably from the college gardens behind the Wren Building. During the Revolution, maps of Williamsburg indicated impressive formal plantings in the college yard. A British garden expert thinks they included a nursery, botanical garden, and beds of herbs and vegetables.

Many campus elms died of blight during the tenure of President Benjamin Ewell, according to Professor Beverley Tucker. A post-Civil War photo shows the front yard denuded. But Ewell planted other trees. Some are thought to be among those now overarching the yard.

During its lean years from 1779 to 1888, the college sold off its original royal acreage until it had only a 17-acre triangle left in 1888, running between Jamestown and Richmond roads. However, President Julian A. C. Chandler bought back many acres, including the farm that once belonged to Captain Robert A. Bright, CSA. It included some 200 acres plus a nineteenth-century brick residence, now housing the Society of the Alumni of William and Mary.

Jefferson, who had befriended the college as alumnus and governor until he created his own University of Virginia, is cited by Professor Mathes as planning a "prospect," or view, from the rear of the Wren Building. Accordingly, Chandler in the 1920s proposed the present Sunken Garden, which was designed by architect Charles M. Robinson in the 1930s after a trip with Chandler to see the sunken gardens at London's Chelsea Hospital.

After Chandler died in 1934, the project was completed by President John Stewart Bryan (1934–42), who contributed 800 boxwood from his Powhatan County farm. They have now grown to large size.

Colonial Williamsburg

The College's front campus, almost denuded by nineteenth-century elm blight, regrew in the twentieth century.

The college yard was landscaped in the 1930s by Arthur Shurcliff, able consultant to Colonial Williamsburg.

Among William and Mary's oldest trees are several live oaks in the original yard, fronting Duke of Gloucester Street. They were taken as seedlings from an earlier live oak noted by mapmaker Robert Beverley in 1678 as forming part of a property boundary of Middle Plantation. Historian Benson Lossing wrote in 1848 that the college was "flanked by stately live oaks, cheering the visitor in winter with evergreen foliage." By 1931 the most ancient tree, called "the Old Monarch of Middle Plantation," had a girth of $9\frac{1}{2}$ feet and was thought to be 275 years old.

Seedlings were taken from the old live oak in 1943 by Professor Donald Davis of the biology department, before it died. They are now growing at the head of the Sunken Garden, around Barrett and Chandler halls, and between Washington and Jefferson halls. In 1948 Professor

Bernice Speese of biology planted other live oaks, among the northernmost growing in the United States.

The 17-acre campus that J. A. C. Chandler took over in 1919 was expanded to 1,200 acres in his 15-year presidency. Today it extends westward nearly a mile on Jamestown Road and half of that on Richmond Road. Close to the western perimeter is Matoaka Lake, which Chandler bought for the college in 1925 from Daniel Selden Jones of Newport News. The lake plus 63 acres cost only $10,000.

The waterway Chandler bought was then called Jones's Millpond, for its millrace fed the mill of the Jones's gristmill, which once ground corn into meal. In earlier times, the Ludwell family had owned the land and mill.

J. A. C. Chandler, called "Jack" by associates, changed "Jones's Millpond" to "Lake Matoaka," just as he renamed the Main Building "the Wren Building." Lake Matoaka and the College Woods were improved in 1933 by the Civilian Conservation Corps, a New Deal project to hire the unemployed. Bridle paths were cut, and a riding stable was built on Jamestown Road, later to become the "Common Glory" ticket office. Today the bridle paths are used by joggers and hikers.

In 1987 the college announced a master plan that would use more of its lake frontage for recreational purposes. The college has sold some remote wooded acreage in "the College Woods" for private development, but all land involved is out of sight of the college and its lake. The lake remains undisturbed.

Besides Martin Mathes and Donald Davis, several other professors have promoted campus beautification. John Millington, a nineteenth-century engineering teacher, was one. Others were Vann F. Garrett, John W. Ritchie, John T. Baldwin, and Bernice Speese.

The rugged, energetic Baldwin was encouraged by President Davis Y. Paschall in the 1960s to collect exotic trees and shrubs for a campus botanical collection. The trees thus planted are visible around the college today: Western white pine, trembling aspen, deodar cedar, Japanese maple, Carolina jasmine, swamp gum, flowering cherry, Leyland cypress, dragon's eye pine, bald cypress, Himalayan pine, West Coast redwood, China fir, and dawn redwood, among others.

John Baldwin was collecting these as early as 1951 including especially the picturesque cryptomeria japonica, which he imported from Japan in 1947. He also helped introduce into the United States the metasequoia, or dawn redwood, a spectacular tree whose needle-like leaves brighten the campus each fall. "It's a prehistoric tree," Baldwin once said, eyes sparkling. Until recently it was known only from fossil remains, estimated to be 13 million years old. But in 1946 live metasequoias were found growing in isolation in Szechuan, China. Professors Baldwin and Speese grew some from seed in 1948 and planted them in Williamsburg. Other exotics and memorial trees have expanded the Baldwin collection.

Professor Mathes likes to quote Jefferson, foremost among William and Mary's former students, to justify the college's tree planting. "The greatest service which can be rendered to any country," Jefferson wrote, "is to add a useful plant to its culture."

Colonial Williamsburg

Arthur Shurcliff landscaped Williamsburg in the 1930s, including the William and Mary yard.

52. *When the Queen Visited*

HISTORIC anniversaries have been the occasion for many celebrations in Williamsburg. Virginians gathered in 1857 to mark the 250th anniversary of the Jamestown settlement. Larger national festivities were the 1881 centenary of Washington's victory at Yorktown and the 1907 and 1957 anniversaries of America's British beginnings at Jamestown. I played a part in 1957 as director of the Jamestown Festival, which began on April 1 of that year and continued till December 1. As an outgrowth, the celebration area called Jamestown Festival Park became a permanent museum.

Of all these anniversary events, the most exciting was the visit of Queen Elizabeth II and Prince Philip to Jamestown and Williamsburg. That day—October 16, 1957—was an unforgettable experience.

The queen's day was the best, even though the president and vice-president of the United States also came to the festival. For that matter, so did most of the 50 governors of the states plus statesmen, diplomats, and Britons. For sentimental reasons I most enjoyed seeing Elizabeth II standing on the shore where John Smith and his fellow voyagers had landed in 1607 to claim Virginia for her predecessor, James I. The queen came for that reason.

It was a short visit, but the royal entourage moved fast and covered Jamestown and Williamsburg in one afternoon and evening. By 10:30 next morning, Elizabeth and Philip were flying off from Patrick Henry Airport in President Eisenhower's plane, Columbine III, to stay at the White House.

That 20-hour visit took two years of preparation. The invitation in 1955 went from the governor to the president and then, after being approved by the State Department and the British Foreign Office, finally to Buckingham Palace. On June 11, 1957, the queen said "Yes."

In 1956 I went with Governor Thomas B. Stanley and festival chairman Lewis McMurran to call on the queen in London, but we couldn't actually mention the invitation then in the works. Only the president could do that. However, Governor Stanley dropped a hint. When the queen told us her mother had enjoyed her visit to Jamestown and Williamsburg in 1954, the governor smiled meaningfully and said "We hope you'll come, too, ma'am."

The queen and prince flew from Canada to Virginia in a British plane that landed at Patrick

Thomas L. Williams

Queen Elizabeth spoke from the Wren Building gallery during her 1957 tour of William and Mary.

Henry Airport. A big red carpet led them from plane to the reception area.

Everybody said the queen was "'prettier than her pictures." Philip, handsome and debonair, walked a few steps behind his wife. With them from London came 37 officials and equerries. I remember especially Foreign Minister Selwyn Lloyd and Ambassador Sir Harold Caccia. Some of the Britons were security men, but they dressed to look like ordinary visitors. The British downplayed police coverage, but U.S. Secret Service and FBI men plus state and local police were densely spread over the queen's route on the Peninsula.

I noticed how simply the queen acknowledged introductions. She simply said "Mr. Governor," "Mr. Ambassador" or "Mr. Chairman," without risking repeating names and getting them wrong. The queen and prince were obviously pleased by the speech that Sam Robinson, the portly black sexton made them when they reached the Jamestown churchyard. The queen was a serious sightseer and took in everything, reading labels and listening to guides all day long. At Jamestown Festival Park she addressed 20,000 people on the mall, reading from her script in a high-pitched voice. She had only been queen a few years then and

Thomas L. Williams

Queen Elizabeth and Prince Philip leave the President's House on their 1957 visit.

she was a little nervous. She was shy but graceful and attractive.

Philip was more relaxed and jocular. He boarded the Susan Constant and stayed so long that the procession fell behind its schedule. The queen apologized for that in a wifely way, explaining that she couldn't do a thing with him when he went aboard a ship.

The royals were especially fascinated by Jim Ware, then one of Jamestown's "red Indians," as the British call our tribesmen, dressed in buckskin and feathers. Lady Rose Baring, one of the queen's ladies-in-waiting, said she descended from Pocahontas, and was therefore glad to see where the Indian princess had come from.

In James Fort at the Festival Park, Prince

Philip was attracted by a costumed interpreter doing punishment in the stocks. "What are you in for?" asked His Royal Highness.

"Scandal-mongering," said the nervous interpreter.

"I wish we could put people in the stocks for that in England," quipped the prince, who gets tired of being gossiped about in British tabloids.

An exciting moment of the Festival Park visit was a fly-over of a half-dozen British and American military planes, which had left the British Isles a few hours earlier. It took pinpoint timing to get them over James Fort at the exact moment the queen and Prince Philip were there, but they did, going on to land at Langley.

From Jamestown the queens' motorcade drove to the College of William and Mary, where they took tea with President and Mrs. Alvin Chandler in the President's House. Then the royal pair went to the Wren Building, where she spoke to a crowd in the college yard.

At College Corner the queen and prince were met by Chairman and Mrs. Winthrop Rockefeller of Colonial Williamsburg and taken by carriage down Duke of Gloucester Street to the Governor's Palace. Soldiers from Fort Knox lined the street in a solid cordon to prevent anyone from frightening the horses which pulled the carriage. Even so, a Secret Service man said carriage rides always made them nervous.

In the Governor's Palace gardens were 1,400 dressed-up Virginians who were neatly lined along garden paths to meet the visitors. As the queen and prince were led down the line, everybody wanted to say something. I heard one Richmond lady tell the prince, "Talking with you, your Highness, I feel I'm British myself."

"I don't know why, madame," he replied. "I'm Greek, you know."

Another guest got out of line after his introduction and reappeared to shake the prince's hand a second time. "Didn't I meet you before?" Philip asked. "That's not cricket," he said. "We'll be here all night!"

After the garden party the queen and prince were taken to Williamsburg Inn, where they had time to bathe and don evening clothes for another reception and a beautiful dinner for 200 guests. The British Embassy had prepared politely worded advice to all guests at dinner that ladies shouldn't wear tiaras or black evening gowns to dine with the queen. None of them did.

After dinner, Governor Stanley introduced Earl Gregg Swem, the wise old librarian of William and Mary, who gave the queen bound copies of 23 Jamestown historical booklets he had edited for the Jamestown Festival. I learned from one of the queen's dinner companions later that she ate little of the breast of chicken, Smithfield ham, green beans, and baked stuffed tomato that the Inn served that night.

I can't speak for Her Majesty, but I was exhausted by the time that day ended. I was just as glad they had to fly to Washington next morning. Just before they left, one sparkish Virginian whispered to Prince Philip that he should stay in town and go dove shooting in that bright October weather.

"I'd love to," said the prince, "but duty calls." With that, Her Majesty Elizabeth, by the grace of God, Queen of England, Defender of the Faith, was off to Washington.

President and Mrs. Thomas Graves with Prince Charles on his 1981 visit to the college.

William and Mary

53. *A Wealth of Museums*

FOR anyone who has lived through the restoration of Williamsburg, the opening in 1985 of the DeWitt Wallace Decorative Arts Gallery was a fulfillment of events that went back nearly 60 years.

They began to crystallize in 1926, when John D. Rockefeller, Jr. gave the go-ahead to rebuild and refurnish some important structures of the eigtheenth-century Virginia capital. Along the way, Williamsburg came to mean more than beautiful buildings and crowds. The town became a hive of eigtheenth-century culture, attracting attention to the Anglo-American past. Rockefeller's initiating generosity attracted other people, rich and poor, who gave Colonial Williamsburg furniture, art, and craft objects related to the town in its glory days.

Now these gifts have come together to form one of the finest collections of period furnishings in America. Though most were given or bought to furnish the exhibition buildings, they long ago outgrew the buildings' capacities. To display 8,000 of them for the public and for specialists' study, Colonial Williamsburg decided to create this museum. DeWitt Wallace, the Reader's Digest founder, gave most of the $17 million to build the unusual, modern building

hidden behind the reconstructed Public Hospital of 1773.

Besides Rockefeller and Wallace, a lot of Williamsburg friends played a part in creating the museum. Some of the finest furniture is the gift of the Miodrag Blagojevichs and the Joseph Hennages, whose names adorn rooms in the gallery. Much of the silver came from Mr. and Mrs. Oliver Ramsey, formerly of Williamsburg.

But the largest gifts were those of the founder Rockefeller and his first wife, Abby Aldrich. The Rockefellers not only sent the first Colonial Williamsburg architect, William Graves Perry, to Europe in the 1930s to buy furnishings for the Governor's Palace, but they made purchases on their own. You can see the Rockefeller's tastes with a ticket that lets you into the Wallace Gallery along with Abby Rockefeller's folk art collection and the couple's erstwhile Bassett Hall, both nearby.

Much of the gallery's collection was acquired by Colonial Williamsburg's three principal curators in its first 60 years: James Cogar, John Graham, and Graham Hood. They built a staff of specialists who planned the gallery to interest laymen and connoisseurs.

The Wallace Gallery, mostly underground,

Colonial Williamsburg

Bassett Hall, Williamsburg home of John D. Rockefeller, Jr., is now a museum house.

was designed by architect Kevin Roche to fit, unseen from the outside, into Williamsburg's historic area. Its top floor is hidden behind a 12-foot brick wall at the rear of the Public Hospital. Yet the interior is well-lighted and ventilated, thanks to atriums that break up the galleries and relax visitors' feet.

To interest casual visitors, the first galleries entered are a mixture of Williamsburg's most celebrated art works. They illustrate what decorative arts are and cover the social changes of Williamsburg's colonial years. For the more dedicated viewer, changing exhibitions come next, introducing themes and personalities touched on in Williamsburg's historic buildings. Finally, a series of smaller "study galleries" deals with each of several major media in

Williamsburg: furniture, ceramics, metals, textiles, prints, and scientific instruments. Here specialists may sit and ponder at leisure.

The Wallace Gallery marks a new era in Restoration history. It recognizes the wide current interest in material culture as a record of social changes. And it brings the Restoration more strongly into the decorative arts field pioneered by Great Britain's Victoria and Albert Museum in 1857. Other major decorative arts collections are in New York's Metropolitan Museum, the Winterthur Museum in Delaware, and the Museum of Early Southern Decorative Arts in Winston-Salem.

The gallery focuses attention on several Virginia artists and craftsmen whom Williamsburg is researching. It shows the Masonic chair built by Benjamin Bucktrout in Williamsburg, acquired by Colonial Williamsburg from a North Carolina owner. Other furniture is from Peter Hay's Williamsburg shop. However, most fine Williamsburg furniture remains English-made, reflecting Americans' use of British importations in colonial years.

In the Masterworks Gallery you will find the Virginia governor's chair, used in the second Williamsburg Capitol after 1753. Flanking it are Allan Ramsey's coronation portrait of King George III of England and his nemesis, George Washington. They suggest the bi-national contents of the gallery.

Also in a central columned atrium, lit by sky-lights, are 150 other objects by English and American artisans from the 1640s to about 1800. Included are several splendid silver objects once owned by England's kings. William Randolph Hearst bought some at auction in London in 1921, and Williamsburg got them in 1938.

The value of the new gallery's exhibits has been estimated at $17 million. Colonial Williamsburg hopes to add appropriate items by gift or purchase as they become available.

Another Williamsburg museum, the Joseph and Margaret Muscarelle Museum of Art at the College of William and Mary opened in 1983. Built with gifts from the Muscarelles and other alumni, it exhibits continuous art shows and provides storage for college paintings going back to a 1732 portrait given by the Earl of Burlington.

Dominated by a triangular exhibit hall with a vast glass solar collector wall facing Jamestown Road, the Muscarelle is reminiscent of the East Wing of Washington's National Gallery. It was designed by Carlton Abbott and Associates of Williamsburg.

Colonial Williamsburg and the college are making reciprocal use of the two museums in teaching art and its history. Curator Graham Hood of Colonial Williamsburg and his staff currently teach courses in William and Mary's Department of Fine Arts, which offers some courses for prospective museum workers.

The galleries reinforce Williamsburg's position as a center for the study of American cultural life. They also strengthen decorative arts research and teaching at the two institutions.

Abby Aldrich Rockefeller Folk Art Center exhibits early American naïve art.

Colonial Williamsburg

54. *A New Crowd of Faces*

SCATTERED through Williamsburg and its suburbs when I came there to live were people who moved to town in the 1920s and '30s to work for John D. Rockefeller, Jr.'s Restoration.

One of them was Robert Webb, who came in 1939 to superintend restoration painting. He was one of the many specialists assembled under Colonel Arthur Woods and Kenneth Chorley, Colonial Williamsburg's first two presidents.

Historic restoration needs trained archaeologists, planners, and experts with other skills. Mr. Rockefeller wanted the best money could buy, sometimes bringing experts from overseas. As a result, Williamsburg became the home of top architects, landscapists, decorators, historians, constructors, and other skilled workers.

Most of that first wave are dead: Rockefeller, W. A. R. Goodwin, Colonel Woods, and Kenneth Chorley among them. So are Vernon Geddy, Sr. and Bela Norton, who were Chorley's top co-workers. Dead, too, are four remarkable Massachusetts contributors: architects William Perry and Singleton Moorehead, landscaper Arthur Shurcliff, and decorator Susan Higginson Nash.

But other early Restorationists are still with us. Retired are architect A. Edwin Kendrew; financial expert I. L. "Rod" Jones; attorney Duncan Cocke; and advertiser Tom McCaskey.

Over on the Eastern Shore lives Jack Upshur, who set up the Craft House. His successor, Harold Sparks, also retired, lives in Williamsburg.

Other retirees here are Mildred Layne and Elizabeth Stubbs, who worked on through most of Carl Humelsine's administration; Shirley Low and Elizabeth Callis, who used to train Colonial Williamsburg's interpreters. Two ladies whom we miss are "Tee" Henderson, who trained all those charming early hostesses, and Louise Fisher, who made Colonial Williamsburg's flower arrangements famous.

Williamsburg's first research director, the Reverend Pierce Middleton, now lives in Annapolis. Mary Mordecai Goodwin, long Colonial Williamsburg's top authority on the town's early people, is fortunately still with us. Also living here is Eleanor Duncan, who has decorated both exhibition buildings and hotels in her long career.

Thinking back, I realize that most who wrote Colonial Williamsburg's first books are dead. Foremost was Rutherfoord Goodwin, eldest son of Dr. Goodwin. Other early Colonial Wil-

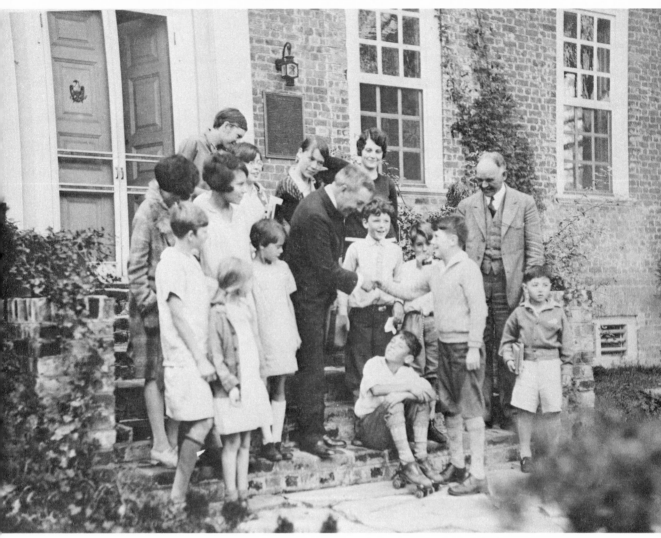

Colonial Williamsburg

John D. Rockefeller, Jr., center, and W. A. R. Goodwin at Wythe House about 1930.

liamsburg authors who have gone are Thomas T. Waterman, Lawrence Kocher, and Howard Dearstyne, who wrote about architecture; Hunter Dickinson Farish and Lester Cappon, who edited eigtheenth-century works; and Gerald Bath, who went from Williamsburg to St. Augustine and then to John B. Stetson University in Florida.

One of the early hotelmen left is Tommy Moyles, who ran the Inn. But I miss his deceased longtime contemporary, Bill Batch-

elder, of the Lodge. And where are all those early waiters and bellmen who graced the Inn and Lodge? I still see some as retirees in Williamsburg, including the Epps brothers and numerous Wallaces.

In the construction field we long ago lost the late Henry Beebe, who left to work for the Rockefeller brothers' far flung resorts. But Otis "Bud" Odell, who went with Beebe, is retired at Westminster-Canterbury at Virginia Beach. Other Colonial Williamsburg constructors like

Charlie Hackett, Lyman Peters, and Granville Patrick, are still with us.

The current enthusiasm for crafts in America should also please everyone who has followed the revival of Williamsburg. Almost from its beginning in 1926, the Restoration planned a series of shops in the Historic Area to revive the skills of eigtheenth-century artisans. They motivated a lot of area craftsmen.

Today, after nineteenth-century industry threatened to stamp out such manual techniques as barrel-making, blacksmithing, basketry, and hand-weaving, every hamlet in America is jumping with craftsmen. Now and then I see them on television, spreading their handiwork for all to see. More than ever, children are being taught to use their hands and their imaginations.

Years ago, Williamsburg's gift and souvenir shops had to import much of their wares from Japan. Today, I'm glad to note, most Williamsburg shops sell more American gifts and souvenirs, some handmade.

I admired many of those craftsmen who came to Williamsburg in the 1930s. One was Paul Griesenauer, a potter who set up shop on his own in the '20s or '30s, making imitations of early Jamestown wares. He called his first, short-lived kiln the James Towne Pottery, and many of its products are prized by owners today. But Paul was too early and too scholarly. His apprentice Jimmy Maloney came later and fared better, expanding his Williamsburg Pottery into today's unbelievable bazaar at Lightfoot.

Max Reig was another pioneer, working as the Restoration's first silversmith. He taught Shirley Robertson, who carried on later in silver and pewter. Now the town has a dozen other silversmiths, some plying their trade for Colonial Williamsburg and others in independent shops.

We've had more cabinetmakers than other craftsmen. One early one was Max Kobelbauer, who ran Colonial Williamsburg's cabinetmakers' shop. Similarly, Don Works, who lived at Five Forks, created mahogany tea caddies and trays, which Colonial Williamsburg sold in its Craft House. Don was a retired Navy commander, and his wife is still with us.

One widely-known arts figure I remember was Billy Bozarth, who conducted periodic antique auctions in Williamsburg, later in Gloucester. In those days prices were far below today's, and many people bought beautiful things for little at Bill's auctions.

Many Virginia craftsmen now prefer to sell directly to the consumer at events like Williamsburg's "Occasion for the Arts," Virginia Beach's art shows, or at weekend flea markets and sidewalk sales in malls and market. Such events are becoming good business. Many towns and shopping centers sponsor them to attract weekend shoppers, always on the lookout for a new place to go, to eat, and to buy.

It's too bad artists and craftsmen have to peddle their stuff, but that's part of being self-employed. Even Picasso had to get out and sell. It didn't hurt him a bit.

55. *The Town That Remembers*

WILLIAMSBURG has four historic offices that reach back to its beginnings: the rector of Bruton Parish, the mayor of Williamsburg, and the rector and the president of the college. Unaccountably, the town has lost track of some of its mayors and the college of some of its rectors. Fires and wars have played havoc with records, but research has turned up some names.

Of all Williamsburg's living relics, Bruton Church is the oldest, going back to the creation of its Anglican parish. One of its early rectors was the Reverend Rowland Jones, Martha Washington's great-grandfather. It has had 27 other ministers through the present one. One of them, W. A. R. Goodwin, served twice. Though the parish dried up badly after half the town moved to Richmond in 1780, Bruton has revived. It is one of the best-known churches in America today, with a large membership.

Seven of Bruton's rectors also were presidents of William and Mary. The college was started as a school to produce Anglican preachers, so its presidents and faculty until the Revolution were Anglican clergy. Even afterwards, it kept a strong Episcopal tone for another century.

The most famous of Bruton's rectors is James Blair, the Scottish minister who persuaded King William and Queen Mary in 1693 to found the college. Next to him, the best known is Dr. Goodwin, who persuaded Rockefeller in 1926 to restore Williamsburg.

After Bruton, the oldest Williamsburg role is the presidency of the college. Among the college's 24 presidents, one served two times. He was Benjamin Ewell. Most of those early preachers who ran William and Mary had rough going. They were Oxford-educated scholars who clashed with Virginia's freedom-minded planters on the Board of Visitors. A surprising number of them died in the President's House and were buried at Bruton or the college.

Not surprisingly, the most influential early William and Mary presidents were the three who served longest: James Blair, 50 years; Bishop James Madison, 35 years; and Benjamin Ewell, 35 years. In recent years, most William and Mary presidents have served about 10 years. It gets harder all the time.

Until recently, nobody had tried to list all the worthies who've been rector of the college—chairman of its Board of Visitors—since it started in 1693. Then Wilford Kale compiled such a

200

Colonial Williamsburg

President and Mrs. Franklin Roosevelt were greeted at Jamestown Church in 1936.

list, which Mary Goodwin and I amplified for publication. It reveals that most of the British governors of Virginia who served in Williamsburg from 1693 till 1769 were rectors of the college: Nicholson, Spotswood, Botetourt, and Fauquier among them.

Many well-known Virginians are also among the 59 known rectors: William Byrd I of Henrico, William Randolph of Henrico, Philip Ludwell II of Greenspring, Peyton Randolph and St. George Tucker of Williamsburg, John Tyler and his father of Charles City, Edmund Ruffin of Prince George, and later J. Brockenbrough Woodward and Herbert Kelly of Newport News.

The mayorship, another longstanding Williamsburg office, was established in 1722 and down to 1989 has had 50 known holders. Several have been well known: John Randolph "the Tory," George Wythe, John Blair, Jr., and John Garland Pollard. It is a post of honor for a town of such small size.

Several researchers have tried to fill out the mayoral record, but there are many gaps from 1722 to 1879. I remember the last six mayors: George Preston Coleman, Channing Hall, Vincent McManus, Henry "Polly" Stryker, Vernon Geddy, Jr., Robert Walker, and John Hodges. They take us back to 1929.

Yes, Williamsburg is a town of continuity. It tries to learn from its past, and sometimes it succeeds.

Association for Preservation of Virginia Antiquities

Carter's Grove on the James was added to Williamsburg's colonial exhibits in 1963.

Acknowledgements

Williamsburg is fortunate in the wealth of its resources for the historian. Both the College of William and Mary and the Colonial Williamsburg Foundation have excellent libraries and archival collections. I have enjoyed their use and the assistance of their staffs since I came to Williamsburg in 1951. This book is a product of that use.

Additionally, the Williamsburg Regional Library has in the past decade become a first-class institution, with a reference library well-equipped to help local historians, like this one. Further afield, I acknowledge help from the Virginia Historical Society library and the Virginia State Library in Richmond and from the reference library of the *Daily Press* in Newport News. Most of the material herein first appeared in the *Daily Press*; some of it in the *Virginia Magazine of History and Biography*.

At the College of William and Mary I owe thanks to William Walker, Kay Domine, Margaret Freeman, and Hope Yelich. I am also appreciative of the continued help I receive from the reference librarians at the Earl Gregg Swem Library. At Colonial Williamsburg I thank Pearce Grove, James Garrett, Suzanne Brown, Albert Louer, Susan Bruno, Hugh DeSamper, Ivor and Audrey Noël Hume, Anne Campana, John Gill, and John Ingram.

At the Institute of Early American History and Culture, I am indebted to my old friends Thad Tate and John Selby.

Other help has come from Virginius Hall of the Virginia Historical Society in Richmond, Dorothy Duffy of Newport News, the Reverend Canon Arthur Pierce Middleton of Annapolis, and Duncan Cocke, Robert Walker, A. Edwin Kendrew, J. Paul Hudson, Leonard Graves, Dr. Janet Kimbrough, Mary Mordecai Goodwin, and Judge Robert Armistead of Williamsburg.

Lastly and especially, I am grateful to my ever-indulgent wife, Betsy Gayle Rouse.

PARKE ROUSE

Bibliography

Ames, Susie: *The Bear and the Cub, the Site of the First English Theatrical Performance in America*, Onancock, Va., 1965

Anonymous: *The Official Guide to Colonial Williamsburg*, Williamsburg, Va., 1988

Bowen, Catherine Drinker: *Miracle at Philadelphia*, Boston, 1986

Carter, Edwin, ed.: *The Journals of Benjamin Latrobe, 1795–1820, from Philadelphia to New Orleans*, New Haven, 1980

Catesby, Mark: *The Natural History of Carolina, Florida, and the Bahama Islands*, 2 v., London, 1748

Coleman, Mary Haldane Begg: *St. George Tucker, Citizen of No Mean City*, Richmond, Va., 1933

Dain, Norman: *Disordered Minds: the First Century of Eastern State Hospital in Williamsburg, Virginia, 1766–1866*, Williamsburg, Va., 1971

Edge, Frederick Milnes: *Major General McClellan and the Campaign on the Yorktown Peninsula*, London, 1865

Gilman, Daniel Coit: *University Problems in the United States*, New York, 1971

Grayson, Cary: *Woodrow Wilson, an Intimate Memoir*, New York, 1960

Harrison, Fairfax: *The Equine FFVs*, Richmond, Va., 1928

Lisle, Laurie: *Portrait of an Artist, A Biography of Georgia O'Keeffe*, New York, 1981

Mathes, Martin: *The Planting of a Campus Tradition*, Williamsburg, Va., 1987

Mackay-Smith, Alexander: *The Colonial Quarter Race Horse*, Richmond, Va., 1983

Middleton, Pierce: *Tobacco Coast, a Maritime History of Chesapeake Bay in the Colonial Era*, Newport News, Va., 1953

Morse, Jedidiah: *American Universal Geography*, 2 v., Boston, 1802-5

Noël Hume, Ivor: *Here Lies Virginia, an Archeologist's View of Colonial Life and History*, New York, 1963

Pollard, John Garland: *A Connotary: Definitions Not Found in Dictionaries, Collected from the Sayings of the Wise and Otherwise*, New York, 1935

Rouse, Parke, Jr.: *A House for a President: 250 Years on the Campus of William and Mary*, Richmond, Va., 1983; *Cows on the Campus: Williamsburg in Bygone Days*, Richmond, Va., 1973; *James Blair of Virginia*, Chapel Hill, 1971

Selby, John: *Dunmore*, Williamsburg, Va., 1977

Simpson, Alan: *The Mysteries of the "Frenchman's Map" of Williamsburg, Virginia*, Williamsburg, Va., 1984

Swem, Earl Gregg: *Brothers of the Spade*, Barre, Vt., 1957

Index